D1561675

DISCARD

The
Mid-Century
American Novel
1935–1965
A Critical History

Twayne's Critical History of the Novel

Herbert Sussman, Series Editor
Northeastern University

The Mid-Century American Novel 1935–1965

Linda Wagner-Martin
The University of North Carolina, Chapel Hill

Twayne Publishers
An Imprint of Simon & Schuster Macmillan
New York

Prentice Hall International
London   Mexico City   New Delhi   Singapore   Sydney   Toronto

3&S 1-31-9792495

813.509
W AG

Twayne's Critical History of the Novel Series

The Mid-Century American Novel, 1935–1965
Linda Wagner-Martin

Copyright © 1997 by Twayne Publishers
All rights reserved. No part of this book may be reproduced
or transmitted in any form or by any means, electronic or
mechanical, including photocopying, recording, or by any
information storage and retrieval system, without permis-
sion in writing from the Publisher.

Twayne Publishers
An Imprint of Simon & Schuster Macmillan
1633 Broadway
New York, New York 10019

Library of Congress Cataloging-in-Publication Data

Wagner-Martin, Linda.
    The mid-century American novel, 1935–1965 / Linda Wagner-Martin.
        p.   cm. — (Twayne's critical history of the novel)
    Includes bibliographical references and index.
    ISBN 0-8057-7860-8 (alk. paper)
        1. American fiction—20th century—History and criticism.
2. American fiction—Minority authors—History and criticism.
3. Popular literature—United States—History and criticism.
4. World War, 1939–1945—Literature and the war.   5. Minorities in
literature.   6. Canon (Literature) I. Title. II. Series.
PS379.W266   1997
813'.509—dc20   96-36725
                                                                                    CIP

The paper used in this publication meets the minimum
requirements of American National Standard for Information Sciences—Permanence of Paper for Printed Library
Materials. ANSI Z39.48-1984. ∞™

10 9 8 7 6 5 4 3 2 1

Printed in the United States of America

For Doug, Karla, and Paul Douglas II
and
Tom and Janet

Contents

Preface

Looking backward, as Edward Bellamy knew more than a century ago, is a reasonable way to see the times in new perspectives. From the vantage point of the 1990s, the sharp lines often said to exist between 1920s modernism and the so-called proletarian writing of the 1930s melt into insubstantial shadows. As Warren I. Susman claimed, "it is all too easy to see a political thirties contrasting dramatically with an apolitical twenties."[1] In 1994, David Minter echoed that conviction: "in terms of relations between politics and literature the thirties differed in significant degree but not in kind from the twenties. . . . the novels of writers like Anderson, cummings, Dos Passos, Fitzgerald, Hemingway, Lewis, and Stein remain deeply if not overtly political."[2] The subject of much American letters is the search for an individuality that does not destroy community: such a theme could not have existed without the inclusion of politics in its largest sense.

Recent assessments of the history of literary movements remind us that the previous demarcation of "high modernist" writing—dominated in America by Ernest Hemingway, T. S. Eliot, John Dos Passos, Jean Toomer, and William Faulkner—contrasted with, or at least set off from, "political" (i.e., Depression) literature—as practiced by James T. Farrell, Albert Halper, Josephine Herbst, Albert Maltz, and John Steinbeck, as well as Hemingway, Dos Passos, and Faulkner—might have been questioned from the start. Obviously, if Hemingway could create one of the quintessential styles of modernism in his stories, in *The Sun Also Rises* (1926), and in *A Farewell to Arms* (1929), his style was not going to change dramatically a few short years later when he tackled such Depression-related themes as economic and social justice in *To Have and Have Not* (1937) and *For Whom the Bell Tolls* (1940).

For John Dos Passos, the kaleidoscopic method he employed in portraying urban citizens in his 1925 *Manhattan Transfer* did not alter in 1930 when he began his depictions of a wider canvas of Americans. His achievement in drawing Bud Korpenning, Joe Harland, Ellen Thatcher, and Jimmy Herf in *Manhattan Transfer* lay beneath his later sketches of Janey, Mac, Eleanor, and J. Ward Moorehouse in *The 42nd Parallel*. What Dos Passos had learned in the brief five years between the two novels was that no meaningful fiction resulted from characters merely moving through plot: his strategy in the first of his *U.S.A.* volumes was to provide what he saw as necessary context. Dos Passos was well educated in both a formal sense and a cultural one: he agreed that "[t]here is no such thing as literature divorced from moral or religious implications."[3] By assembling a quantity of historical and sociological information and arranging it into the varied structures *U.S.A.* made possible, he hoped to write instructive novels. Pushing the borders of the written text early in the decade that became famous for its documentary photographs and reportage, Dos Passos was both thoroughly modernist and thoroughly political.

I have written elsewhere[4] of the ways in which Faulkner's writing can be read as illustrative of the shifts in mood and circumstances in American culture from the 1920s through the 1930s. His fascination with the meaning of community, and his continuous interrogation of the ways in which individuals related (or failed to relate) to that larger entity, provided the theme for much of his major fiction—not only *Light in August* (1931) and *Absalom, Absalom!* (1936) but also *The Unvanquished* (1938), *The Wild Palms* (1939), *Go Down, Moses* (1942), *A Fable* (1954), and the Snopes trilogy (*The Hamlet* [1940], *The Town* [1957], and *The Mansion* [1959]).*

F. Scott Fitzgerald is less often caught in the dissonance between what he wrote in the 1920s and work that appeared in the 1930s, but there is a wide difference between his 1925 *The Great Gatsby*, with its multivalent themes, and his 1934 *Tender Is the Night*, with its much harsher view of the culture that helped create its protagonists. Unlike Sinclair Lewis, the first American novelist to win the Nobel Prize for Literature (in 1931), Fitzgerald was responsive to currents of cultural change. Even though Lewis finally tried to assess the

---

*My earlier study, *The Modern American Novel, 1914–1945*, is a foundation for this volume; it is also a voice in the continuing discourse about canon and periodization. Since its writing in the late 1980s, criticism of American letters has changed greatly, and any reader's understanding of these patterns in fiction has been enriched by those changes. The books overlap in part because of the obvious repetition of the years 1935 to 1945 in each study.

changes in the fabric of American life in *It Can't Happen Here* (1935), readers found the passive Doremus Jessup a tepid spokesman for the traumatic thirties. In fact, Lewis's omnivorous coverage of American characters identified by their occupations seldom varied. *Arrowsmith* (1925), *Dodsworth* (1929), and even *Elmer Gantry* (1927) were copies of the pattern that had made *Babbitt* (1922) so popular. Perhaps Lewis's appeal for readers the world over lay in precisely this predictability.

Chronology

This chronology gives some sense of the intense activity in American letters from the mid-thirties to the mid-sixties. For reasons of space, not every work by each author appears.

1935   William Faulkner, *Pylon.* Sherwood Anderson, *Puzzled America.* John Steinbeck, *Tortilla Flat.* Albert Maltz, *Black Pit.* Nelson Algren, *Somebody in Boots.* Ellen Glasgow, *Vein of Iron.* Tom Kromer, *Waiting for Nothing.* Sinclair Lewis, *It Can't Happen Here.* James T. Farrell, *Studs Lonigan.* Mari Sandoz, *Old Jules.* Clara Weatherwax, *Marching! Marching!.* Zora Neale Hurston, *Mules and Men.* Wallace Stevens, *Ideas of Order.* Ezra Pound, *Make It New, Jefferson and/or Mussolini.* Muriel Rukeyser, *Theory of Flight.* T. S. Eliot, *Murder in the Cathedral.* Langston Hughes, *Mulatto.* Clifford Odets, *Waiting for Lefty, Awake and Sing!.* Edwin Arlington Robinson dies. Federal Writers' Project, 1935–1939.

1936   John Dos Passos, *The Big Money.* Arna Bontemps, *Black Thunder.* John Steinbeck, *In Dubious Battle.* Kay Boyle, *Death of a Man.* Henry Miller, *Black Spring.* James Rorty, *Where Life Is Better.* William Faulkner, *Absalom, Absalom!.* Meridel LeSueur, *The Girl.* Djuna Barnes, *Nightwood.* Margaret Mitchell, *Gone with the Wind.* Harriette Arnow, *Mountain Path.* James M. Cain, *Double Indemnity.* Thomas Bell, *All Brides Are Beautiful.* Robert Frost, *A Further Range.* Carl Sandburg, *The People, Yes.* Eugene O'Neill receives the Nobel Prize in Literature; Federal Theatre Project is initiated. Spanish Civil War begins (continuing until 1939). Federico García Lorca dies.

1937   Ernest Hemingway, *To Have and Have Not.* Albert Halper, *The Chute.* John Steinbeck, *The Red Pony, Of Mice and Men.* Waters E. Turpin, *These Low Grounds.* Zora Neale Hurston, *Their Eyes Were Watching God.* John P. Marquand, *The Late George Apley.* William Carlos Williams, *White Mule.* Younghill Kang, *East Goes West.* Gertrude Stein, *Everybody's*

Autobiography. Evelyn Scott, *Bread and Sword.* Lin Yutang, *My Country and My People.* Erskine Caldwell and Margaret Bourke-White, *You Have Seen Their Faces.* Wallace Stevens, *The Man with the Blue Guitar.* Edith Wharton dies.

1938   Richard Wright, *Uncle Tom's Children.* John Dos Passos, *U.S.A.* Robert Sherwood, *Abe Lincoln in Illinois.* John Crowe Ransom, *The World's Body.* May Sarton, *The Single Hound.* Thornton Wilder, *Our Town.* Edith Wharton, *The Buccaneers.* William Rollins Jr., *The Wall of Men.* e. e. cummings, *Collected Poems.* Pearl Buck receives the Nobel Prize in Literature; Thomas Wolfe dies.

1939   William Faulkner, *The Wild Palms.* Katherine Anne Porter, *Pale Horse, Pale Rider.* John Steinbeck, *The Grapes of Wrath.* Josephine Herbst, *Rope of Gold.* Raymond Chandler, *The Big Sleep.* Ruth McKenney, *Industrial Valley.* Pietro Di Donato, *Christ in Concrete.* Henry Miller, *Tropic of Capricorn.* Anais Nin, *The Winter of Artifice.* Nathanael West, *The Day of the Locust.* Dorothy Parker, *Here Lies.* Lillian Hellman, *The Little Foxes.* Edna St. Vincent Millay, *Huntsman, What Quarry?.* Dorothea Lange and Paul S. Taylor, *An American Exodus.* William Butler Yeats, Ford Madox Ford, and Sigmund Freud die. World War II begins with Germany's invasion of Poland.

1940   Richard Wright, *Native Son.* Carson McCullers, *The Heart Is a Lonely Hunter.* Thomas Wolfe, *You Can't Go Home Again.* Albert Maltz, *The Underground Stream.* Caroline Slade, *The Triumph of Willie Pond.* Ernest Hemingway, *For Whom the Bell Tolls.* Raymond Chandler, *Farewell, My Lovely.* Glenway Wescott, *The Pilgrim Hawk.* Albert Halper, *Sons of the Fathers.* Martha Gellhorn, *A Stricken Field.* Ezra Pound, *The Cantos.* Langston Hughes, *The Big Sea.* Janet Flanner, *An American in Paris.* Eugene O'Neill, *Long Day's Journey into Night.* Willa Cather, *Sapphira and the Slave Girl.* William Saroyan, *My Name Is Aram.* Elizabeth Madox Roberts, *Song in the Meadow.* F. Scott Fitzgerald, Hamlin Garland, Nathanael West, and Emma Goldman die.

1941   F. Scott Fitzgerald, *The Last Tycoon.* James Agee and Walker Evans, *Let Us Now Praise Famous Men.* Marianne Moore, *What Are Years?.* Lillian Hellman, *Watch on the Rhine.* Eudora

Welty, *A Curtain of Green*. Caroline Gordon, *Green Centuries*. Theodore Roethke, *Open House*. Paul Green, *Native Son* (stage adaptation). Ellen Glasgow, *In This Our Life*. Robinson Jeffers, *Be Angry at the Sun*. Carson McCullers, *Reflections in a Golden Eye*. Budd Schulberg, *What Makes Sammy Run?*. Vladimir Nabokov, *The Real Life of Sebastian Knight*. Sherwood Anderson and Elizabeth Madox Roberts die. The U.S. enters World War II after the Japanese attack Pearl Harbor.

1942　William Faulkner, *Go Down, Moses*. Kenneth Burke, *The White Oxen*. Nelson Algren, *Never Come Morning*. Ruth Suckow, *New Hope*. Eudora Welty, *The Robber Bridegroom*. Kay Boyle, *Primer for Combat*. John Steinbeck, *The Moon Is Down*. Mary McCarthy, *The Company She Keeps*. Wright Morris, *My Uncle Dudley*. John Hersey, *Men on Bataan*. William Saroyan, *The Human Comedy*. Wallace Stevens, *Notes toward a Supreme Fiction*. Robert Frost, *A Witness Tree*. Margaret Walker, *For My People*. Thornton Wilder, *The Skin of Our Teeth*. Pearl Buck, *Dragon Seed*. James Thurber, *My World— and Welcome to It*. Marjorie Kinnan Rawlings, *Cross Creek*.

1943　John Dos Passos, *Number One*. Wallace Stegner, *The Big Rock Candy Mountain*. Carlos Bulosan, *The Voice of Bataan*. Ayn Rand, *The Fountainhead*. T. S. Eliot, *Four Quartets*. Kenneth Fearing, *Afternoon of a Pawnbroker*. Robert Penn Warren, *At Heaven's Gate*. James T. Farrell, *My Days of Anger*. Weldon Kees, *The Last Man*. Betty Smith, *A Tree Grows in Brooklyn*. Eudora Welty, *The Wide Net*. Jane Bowles, *Two Serious Ladies*.

1944　Saul Bellow, *Dangling Man*. Lillian Smith, *Strange Fruit*. Carlos Bulosan, *Laughter of My Father*. William Carlos Williams, *The Wedge*. Lillian Hellman, *The Searching Wind*. John Hersey, *A Bell for Adano*. John Steinbeck, *Cannery Row*. Caroline Gordon, *The Women on the Porch*. Harry Brown, *A Walk in the Sun*. Jean Stafford, *Boston Adventure*. Anais Nin, *Under a Glass Bell*. H. D., *The Walls Do Not Fall*. Ernie Pyle, *Brave Men*. Karl Shapiro, *V-Letter and Other Poems*.

1945　Gertrude Stein, *Wars I Have Seen*. Richard Wright, *Black Boy*. Chester Himes, *If He Hollers Let Him Go*. F. Scott Fitzgerald, *The Crack-Up*. H. D., *Tribute to the Angels*. Robert Frost, *A Masque of Reason*. Gwendolyn Brooks, *A Street in Bronzeville*.

Tennessee Williams, *The Glass Menagerie*. Eudora Welty, *Delta Wedding*. Randall Jarrell, *Little Friend, Little Friend*. Josephina Niggli, *Mexican Village*. Betty MacDonald, *The Egg and I*. Jessamyn West, *The Friendly Persuasion*. Ellen Glasgow and Theodore Dreiser die. World War II ends after the U.S. atomic bombing of Hiroshima and Nagasaki.

1946   Robert Penn Warren, *All the King's Men*. Ann Petry, *The Street*. Josephine Johnson, *Wildwood*. Elizabeth Bishop, *North & South*. Pearl Buck, *Pavilion of Women*. Gore Vidal, *Williwaw*. Robinson Jeffers, *Medea*. Carson McCullers, *The Member of the Wedding*. Robert Lowell, *Lord Weary's Castle*. Eugene O'Neill, *The Iceman Cometh*. Gertrude Stein, *Brewsie and Willie*. William Carlos Williams, *Paterson*, vol. I. Gertrude Stein dies.

1947   Jean Stafford, *The Mountain Lion*. Saul Bellow, *The Victim*. Frank Yerby, *The Foxes of Harrow*. Willard Motley, *Knock on Any Door*. Ann Petry, *Country Life*. Fannie Hurst, *Hands of Veronica*. John Steinbeck, *The Pearl, The Wayward Bus*. Arthur Miller, *All My Sons*. Tennessee Williams, *A Streetcar Named Desire*. Laura Z. Hobson, *Gentleman's Agreement*. Richard Wilbur, *The Beautiful Changes*. Vance Bourjaily, *The End of My Life*. John Horne Burns, *The Gallery*. James A. Michener, *Tales of the South Pacific*. Mickey Spillane, *I, the Jury*. Willa Cather dies.

1948   Irwin Shaw, *The Young Lions*. Truman Capote, *Other Voices, Other Rooms*. Norman Mailer, *The Naked and the Dead*. Horace McCoy, *Kiss Tomorrow Goodbye*. Thomas Merton, *The Seven Storey Mountain*. Ezra Pound, *The Pisan Cantos*. Betty Smith, *Tomorrow Will Be Better*. Gore Vidal, *The City and the Pillar*. Frederick Buechner, *The Return of Ansel Gibbs*. William Faulkner, *Intruder in the Dust*. Lin Yutang, *Chinatown Family*. T. S. Eliot is awarded the Nobel Prize in Literature.

1949   Paul Bowles, *The Sheltering Sky*. Nelson Algren, *The Man with the Golden Arm*. John Hawkes, *The Cannibal*. Ross MacDonald (Kenneth Millar), *The Moving Target*. Gwendolyn Brooks, *Annie Allen*. Arthur Miller, *Death of a Salesman*. Shirley Jackson, *The Lottery*. Lillian Smith, *Killers of the Dream*. Eudora Welty, *The Golden Apples*. William Faulkner, *Knight's Gambit*.

1950   Paul Bowles, *The Delicate Prey*. Ray Bradbury, *The Martian Chronicles*. T. S. Eliot, *The Cocktail Party*. John Hersey, *The Wall*. Anzia Yezierska, *Red Ribbon on a White Horse*. Ernest Hemingway, *Across the River and into the Trees*. Conrad Aiken, *Short Stories*. John Dos Passos, *The Prospect before Us*. Carl Sandburg, *Complete Poems*. Wallace Stegner, *The Women on the Wall*. Wallace Stevens, *The Auroras of Autumn*. Langston Hughes, *Simple Speaks His Mind*. William Inge, *Come Back, Little Sheba*. William Faulkner, *Collected Stories*. William Faulkner is awarded the Nobel Prize in Literature. Edna St. Vincent Millay and Edgar Lee Masters die. U.S. troops invade North Korea; McCarthy investigations begin.

1951   James Jones, *From Here to Eternity*. Herman Wouk, *The Caine Mutiny*. Rachel Carson, *The Sea around Us*. Shelby Foote, *Love in a Dry Season*. Carson McCullers, *The Ballad of the Sad Cafe*. Norman Mailer, *Barbary Shore*. Adrienne Rich, *A Change of World*. J. D. Salinger, *The Catcher in the Rye*. Shirley Jackson, *Hangsaman*. William Carlos Williams, *The Autobiography*. Hortense Calisher, *In the Absence of Angels*. William Faulkner, *Requiem for a Nun*. Sinclair Lewis dies.

1952   Ralph Ellison, *Invisible Man*. Flannery O'Connor, *Wise Blood*. Claire Morgan (Patricia Highsmith), *The Price of Salt*. Ernest Hemingway, *The Old Man and the Sea*. Edna Ferber, *Giant*. Bernard Malamud, *The Natural*. Elizabeth Spencer, *This Crooked Way*. Jean Stafford, *The Catherine Wheel*. John Steinbeck, *East of Eden*. Kurt Vonnegut Jr., *Player Piano*.

1953   James Baldwin, *Go Tell It on the Mountain*. Arthur Miller, *The Crucible*. Ann Petry, *The Narrows*. J. D. Salinger, *Nine Stories*. Saul Bellow, *The Adventures of Augie March*. John Cheever, *The Enormous Radio*. William Inge, *Picnic*. Gwendolyn Brooks, *Maud Martha*. Monica Sone, *Nisei Daughter*. Richard Wright, *The Outsider*. Leon Uris, *Battle Cry*. Eugene O'Neill and John Horne Burns die. The Korean War armistice is signed.

1954   Raymond Chandler, *The Long Goodbye*. William Faulkner, *A Fable*. Richard Wright, *Savage Holiday*. Randall Jarrell, *Pictures from an Institution*. Harriette Arnow, *The Dollmaker*. Eudora Welty, *The Ponder Heart*. William Carlos Williams, *The Desert Music*. Louise Bogan, *Collected Poems*. Ellen Glasgow,

The Woman Within. Shirley Jackson, *The Bird's Nest*. Archibald MacLeish, *Songs for Eve*. Ernest Hemingway receives the Nobel Prize in Literature.

1955   Tennessee Williams, *Cat on a Hot Tin Roof*. Anne Morrow Lindbergh, *Gift from the Sea*. Norman Mailer, *The Deer Park*. Vladimir Nabokov, *Lolita*. Flannery O'Connor, *A Good Man Is Hard to Find*. J. P. Donleavy, *The Ginger Man*. William Gaddis, *The Recognitions*. William Inge, *Bus Stop*. Gertrude Stein, *Painted Lace and Other Pieces*. Sloan Wilson, *The Man in the Gray Flannel Suit*.

1956   Nelson Algren, *A Walk on the Wild Side*. Pearl Buck, *Imperial Woman*. Elizabeth Spencer, *The Voice at the Back Door*. William Styron, *The Long March*. James Baldwin, *Giovanni's Room*. John Barth, *The Floating Opera*. John Berryman, *Homage to Mistress Bradstreet*. Allen Ginsberg, *Howl and Other Poems*. Saul Bellow, *Seize the Day*. Eileen Chang, *The Naked Earth*. Grace Metalious, *Peyton Place*.

1957   William Faulkner, *The Town*. Bernard Malamud, *The Assistant*. Vladimir Nabokov, *Pnin*. Ayn Rand, *Atlas Shrugged*. Isaac Bashevis Singer, *Gimpel the Fool*. Jack Kerouac, *On the Road*. Denise Levertov, *Here and Now*. James Agee, *A Death in the Family*. John Okada, *No-No Boy*. Ann Bannon, *Odd Girl Out*. Chester Himes, *For Love of Imabell (A Rage in Harlem)*.

1958   Bernard Malamud, *The Magic Barrel*. Willard Motley, *Let No Man Write My Epitaph*. Theodore Roethke, *Words for the Wind*. Thomas Berger, *Crazy in Berlin*. William Carlos Williams, *Paterson*, vol V. Shirley Ann Grau, *The Hard Blue Sky*. Jack Kerouac, *The Dharma Bums*. John Barth, *The End of the Road*.

1959   Peter Taylor, *Happy Families Are All Alike*. John Hersey, *The War Lover*. Lorraine Hansberry, *A Raisin in the Sun*. William Faulkner, *The Mansion*. Evan S. Connell Jr., *Mrs. Bridge*. Kurt Vonnegut Jr., *The Sirens of Titan*. Robert Penn Warren, *The Cave*. William S. Burroughs, *Naked Lunch*. James A. Michener, *Hawaii*. Saul Bellow, *Henderson the Rain King*. James Purdy, *Malcolm*. Grace Paley, *The Little Disturbances of Man*. Philip Roth, *Goodbye, Columbus*. Paule Marshall, *Brown Girl, Brownstones*.

1960   Flannery O'Connor, *The Violent Bear It Away*. John Barth, *The Sot-Weed Factor*. E. L. Doctorow, *Welcome to Hard Times*. H. D., *Bid Me to Live*. James Purdy, *The Nephew*. William Styron, *Set This House on Fire*. John Updike, *Rabbit, Run*. Charles Olson, *The Maximus Poems*. Harper Lee, *To Kill a Mockingbird*. Elizabeth Spencer, *The Light in the Piazza*. Richard Wright and John P. Marquand die.

1961   Shirley Ann Grau, *The House on Coliseum Street*. Robert A. Heinlein, *Stranger in a Strange Land*. Joseph Heller, *Catch-22*. Arthur Miller, *The Misfits*. Walker Percy, *The Moviegoer*. Kurt Vonnegut Jr., *Mother Night*. Edward Lewis Wallant, *The Pawnbroker*. J. D. Salinger, *Franny and Zooey*. John Dos Passos, *Midcentury*. Paule Marshall, *Soul Clap Hands and Sing*. John A. Williams, *Night Song*. Larry McMurtry, *Horseman, Pass By*. Henry Miller, *Tropic of Cancer*. Tillie Olsen, *Tell Me a Riddle*. Ernest Hemingway, James Thurber, and Dashiell Hammett die.

1962   James Baldwin, *Another Country*. Edward Albee, *Who's Afraid of Virginia Woolf?*. Rachel Carson, *The Silent Spring*. William Faulkner, *The Reivers*. James Jones, *The Thin Red Line*. Alison Lurie, *Love and Friendship*. Vladimir Nabokov, *Pale Fire*. Katherine Anne Porter, *Ship of Fools*. Wilma Dykeman, *The Tall Woman*. Ken Kesey, *One Flew over the Cuckoo's Nest*. Kay Boyle, *Collected Poems*. J. F. Powers, *Morte d'Urban*. Reynolds Price, *A Long and Happy Life*. John Hawkes, *The Cannibal*. John Steinbeck is awarded the Nobel Prize in Literature. William Faulkner, e. e. cummings, and Robinson Jeffers die. U.S. troops are sent to Vietnam.

1963   Mary McCarthy, *The Group*. Joan Didion, *Run River*. J. P. Donleavy, *A Singular Man*. Susan Sontag, *The Benefactor*. John Updike, *The Centaur*. Kurt Vonnegut Jr., *Cat's Cradle*. Joyce Carol Oates, *By the North Gate*. Sylvia Plath, *The Bell Jar*. John Rechy, *City of Night*. Thomas Pynchon, *V.* James Baldwin, *The Fire Next Time*. Betty Friedan, *The Feminine Mystique*. Linda Ty-Casper, *The Transparent Sun and Other Stories*. Jack Kerouac, *Visions of Gerard*. Ella Winter, *And Not to Yield*. President John F. Kennedy is assassinated. Robert Frost, Sylvia Plath, Theodore Roethke, William Carlos Williams, and Clifford Odets die.

1964   Joyce Carol Oates, *With Shuddering Fall*. Hubert Selby Jr., *Last Exit to Brooklyn*. Anne Tyler, *If Morning Ever Comes*. Adrienne Kennedy, *Funnyhouse of a Negro*. Ernest Hemingway, *A Moveable Feast*. LeRoi Jones, *Dutchman, The Slave*. Ken Kesey, *Sometimes a Great Notion*. Shirley Ann Grau, *The Keepers of the House*. Donald Barthelme, *Come Back, Dr. Caligari*. Saul Bellow, *Herzog*. Thomas Berger, *Little Big Man*. Richard Brautigan, *A Confederate General from Big Sur*. William S. Burroughs, *Nova Express*. Bruce Jay Friedman, *A Mother's Kisses*. Jane Rule, *Desert of the Heart*. Ernest J. Gaines, *Catherine Carmier*. Flannery O'Connor and Rachel Carson die.

1965   May Sarton, *Mrs. Stevens Hears the Mermaids Singing*. Thomas Wolfe, *The Lost Boy*. Jerzy Kosinski, *The Painted Bird*. Cormac McCarthy, *The Orchard Keeper*. *The Autobiography of Malcolm X*. Peter Matthiessen, *At Play in the Fields of the Lord*. Flannery O'Connor, *Everything That Rises Must Converge*. Margaret Walker, *Jubilee*. Maureen Howard, *Bridgeport Bus*. Malcolm X is assassinated. T. S. Eliot and Randall Jarrell die.

1

Currents in Despair

Not only did Hemingway, Fitzgerald, Dos Passos, Lewis, and Faulkner themselves continue writing into the 1930s (and beyond), but their visibility as premier writers influenced 1930s literature in countless other ways. James T. Farrell, Erskine Caldwell, Josephine Herbst, Nelson Algren, James M. Cain, John Steinbeck, Richard Wright, Albert Maltz, Arna Bontemps, Mike Gold, Ella Winter—who of the best-known 1930s writers had not learned to write by reading Hemingway, Lewis, Faulkner? The qualities that had come to be associated with the startling phenomenon of American modernist writing, less erudite and more honest than its British counterpart, were already prized, already adopted, by fledgling writers. In their choice of direct and simple language (what William Carlos Williams was calling "the American idiom"), of straightforward stories told in stark narrative lines, and with an emphasis on concrete, visualized detail, these younger writers accepted and used the distinctive style of modernist writing.

There was a difference, however, one that Hemingway felt when he published *To Have and Have Not* in 1937. Whereas many of the post–World War I modernists had felt that the stylized presentation of the contemporary self was enough for art to accomplish, many of these 1930s writers (as well as the modernists who tried to write for the 1930s audience) wanted to turn their stripped-down talent to a somewhat more immediate use: they wanted to reach the real American reader who was, more than likely, a pragmatic reader—looking for interesting stories, or for interesting characters, or for narratives germane to the times. Demand for literature as escape still lived, but it was now balanced with a demand for literature as answer to the pervasive social problems of the 1930s. But first, literature felt compelled to simply describe those problems. Too many readers (people who could still afford to purchase books) did not understand what had happened to more than half the citizens of this great democracy.

Few readers can think of the 1930s in the United States without equating that decade with the economic debacle of the Great

Depression. Between October 24 and November 10, 1929, "thirty billion dollars in paper value had vanished. . . . The whole credit structure of the American economy had been shaken up more severely than anybody then dared guess."[1] According to Frederick Lewis Allen, Wall Street had lost all financial authority; by mid-1932, U.S. industry was operating at less than half its 1929 volume. Wages were 60% less than those paid in 1929, so there was significantly less currency in circulation. The poverty of U.S. citizens, however, was "oddly invisible" because people pretended to be secure. For a country that had long equated financial value with moral behavior, such a reasonless monetary disaster threatened the roots of personal belief. As Allen notes, millions of people were "marked—inwardly—for the rest of their lives."[2]

The Fiction of Hunger

Halford E. Luccock believes that the "emergence of hunger into [American] literature . . . is one of the major differences between the 1930s and the 1920s."[3] What the topic of hunger meant for the writer was that fiction had to be devised about different kinds of characters—hungry ones. Even in the days of Mark Twain's poor, or Horatio Alger's strivers, or Rebecca Harding Davis's ironworkers, writers did not emphasize sheer desperate hunger: in the 1930s, in contrast, many plots were built around food—obtaining it (through barter, work, or theft), enjoying it, and viewing its possession as an index of moral worth.

Much fiction of the 1930s can, in fact, be judged by its effectiveness in describing both actual hunger and the physical work that enabled people to buy food. Separate from any political agenda (and far from being anti-American or either socialist or Communist), work by writers as diverse as Erskine Caldwell, Tillie Lerner Olsen, James Rorty, Arna Bontemps, Sherwood Anderson, Albert Maltz, and Meridel LeSueur used the theme of hunger to evoke sympathetic responses. Such novels as Jack Conroy's *The Disinherited* and Tom Kromer's *Waiting for Nothing* have little narrative except the appeasement of characters' hunger.

It is a commonplace of literary history that many writers were moved to respond to the tragedy of the Depression in reportage and other nonfiction prose. Incredulous that a country known for its plenty could be filled with such physical despair, established writers like Sherwood Anderson, Edmund Wilson, Theodore Dreiser, and Nathan Asch traveled through the country, writing columns as well as book-length narratives about this newly impoverished land. Most of these nonfiction writers used the dramatic ploy of picturing characters as hungry: to starve in America was inconceivable. In the introduction to his 1935 *Puzzled America*, Sherwood Anderson notes, "There are, everywhere in America, these people now out of work. There are women and children hungry and others without enough clothes. . . . "[4]

A few pages later, he nails the reader's sympathy down hard with his image of a person foraging for edible garbage: "—it has happened to me—this would be after dark at night—I see a man lurking in an open place between two buildings. I stop and look. He is pawing over the contents of a garbage can." Because Anderson's middle-class reader surely cannot understand what the man is doing, the author continues, "It does happen, things like that, to Americans, people in this big rich place. It happens that men have no shoes, that men here who have families go home at night to hungry, crying children. . . . and it is not true, dear reader, that these men, these Americans, are necessarily in any way inferior to you or to me."[5]

Didactic as Anderson's message is, the metaphor of hunger occurs in writing that is not ostensibly about this aspect of the Depression. In their cowritten nonfiction work, *They Seek a City* (later titled *Anyplace But Here*), Jack Conroy and Arna Bontemps use the image of six adolescent boys—three black, three white—riding the rails northward from the South to reach Detroit, where they hope to get work in the auto plants. Here in a "hobo jungle," the luminous image of community is a meal:

All had been foraging for food and were now pooling their combined catch for a "mulligan": a ham bone, a can of tomatoes for which one had been compelled to yield a dime, some scraps of bacon, green corn from a near-by field.[6]

Journalist Meridel LeSueur, too, centers her description of women waiting for work in an employment bureau waiting room with the same penetrating detail, "We sit here every day, waiting for a job. There are no jobs. Most of us have had no breakfast. Some have had scant rations for over a year."[7] She also editorializes, knowing that she writes (early in the 1930s) for readers who do not understand much about being hungry: "Hunger makes a human being lapse into a state of lethargy, especially city hunger . . . the timid crawl the streets, hunger like a beak of a terrible bird at the vitals."[8]

LeSueur brings food-related details into each of her columns about women trying to survive Depression conditions. There is the nameless woman with no income who eats only a cracker a day, making no trouble, hoping only not to be thrown out of the room she cannot pay for. There is a seemingly harsh exchange between a young woman, out of work for eight months, who demands a job from the YMCA woman who reprimands her for her unshined shoes—cruel and unreachable because she knows the girl is starving: "facing each other in a rage both helpless, helpless."[9] There is the teacher who tries to get work from the welfare agency because she has no money at all, but because she still wears a suit and is a professional, she is turned away. So disoriented from her constant hunger that she cannot tell a convincing story about how she has been living, she realizes she will never receive help, and after that realization, she walks to a nearby bridge and—simply—jumps to her death. As LeSueur had written elsewhere, "Not one of them [the out-of-work women] but looks forward to starvation for the coming winter. . . . Not one of these women but knows that despite years of labor there is only starvation, humiliation in front of them."[10] By choosing an ironic title, "Women on the Breadlines," for her collected columns, LeSueur makes the searing point that even the hungriest of women were seldom included in food handouts or shelter programs sponsored by charities or governments.

Lewis Adamic's nonfiction *My America, 1928–1938*, takes a more statistical approach to describing the ravages of the Depression. In reporting that there were 82 breadlines in New York City in January of 1931, serving approximately 85,000 meals a day, he chooses to give his readers the actual items the men waiting for that food would have received. For breakfast, oatmeal and coffee or rolls and coffee; for the other meals, "bread, soup, coffee; stew and bread; cheese or meat sandwiches and coffee; beans, bread, and coffee."[11] Adamic itemizes to counter the anger of middle-class readers who—insulated from such poverty—were critical of relief measures.

By 1936, when he published his reportage as a book titled *Where Life Is Better: An Unsentimental American Journey*, James Rorty used the by-now-accepted fact of pervasive hunger to characterize the people he saw as eternally optimistic. (In 1935, 22 million Americans were on relief;[12] hunger was hardly rare.) Still hopeful, many of the people he had met as he traveled the country believed that their lives would turn around, that they too would be able to have families and homes. Rorty's cynical translation for *hope* is *fantasy*. As he writes, "I encountered nothing in 15,000 miles of travel that disgusted and appalled me so much as this American addiction to makebelieve. Apparently, not even empty bellies can cure it."[13]

Fiction of the times made even better use of the painful phenomenon. Erskine Caldwell's short stories "Rachel" and "Daughter" marked him for a kind of fame different from the low comedy of his early novels, *God's Little Acre* and *Tobacco Road*. The proud child who dies after eating poisoned food from her boyfriend's garbage can hovers in memory,[14] as does the jailed father who has killed his child with a shotgun: "Daughter said she was hungry, and I just couldn't stand it no longer. I just couldn't stand to hear her say it." The contextualization Caldwell works into the latter, brief story lets Jim, a man respected by his community, explain further: "I've been working all year and I made enough for all of us to eat. . . . I made enough working on shares, but they came and took it all away from me. . . . They just came and took it all off. Then daughter woke up again this morning saying she was hungry, and I just couldn't stand it no longer. . . . I just couldn't stand it no longer."[15]

Jim's deranged bewilderment—his need to stop his child's misery, and his own—is a variation on a narrative familiar to the 1930s: that of men who cannot understand why they have failed. The paternalistic culture which set the male breadwinner at the head of the family, coupled with the materialism of the American dream of success, created an imbroglio that male egos could not untangle. To be without money and food was to have failed.

Having taken a degree in philosophy from Columbia University as well as playwriting courses at Yale, Albert Maltz learned that the trope of hunger worked better than abstract theorizing. In "The Happiest Man on Earth," Maltz created a starving young husband who walks through two states to beg his brother-in-law for work driving a nitroglycerin truck, discounting all warnings about the danger of that position. Even more poignant is the miner in "Man on a Road" who leaves his wife in order to go away and die, alone, of silicosis—thereby giving her and his children what little they have. Here the image of hunger bonds the driver with the miserable hitchhiker. Upset because his passenger is almost comatose, the driver asks him to have a cup of coffee:

"Yes," he replied, "thank you, friend."
The "thank you" told me a lot. I knew from the way he said it that he wanted the coffee but couldn't pay for it; that he had taken my offer to be one of hospitality and was grateful. I was happy I had asked him.
We went inside. For the first time since I had come upon him . . . he seemed human. He didn't talk, but he didn't slip inside himself either. He just sat down at the counter and waited for his coffee. When it came, he drank it slowly, holding the cup in both hands as though to warm them.
When he had finished, I asked him if he wouldn't like a sandwich. He turned around to me and smiled. It was a very gentle, a very patient smile. His big, lumpy face seemed to light up with it and become understanding and sweet and gentle.
The smile shook me all through. It didn't warm me—it made me feel sick inside.[16]

Maltz's reportorial narrative places the reader in the same position as the driver—better off financially, unable to understand the reason for the protagonist's withdrawal. When the silent man on the road asks the driver to copy his letter to his wife, a letter in which he explains that he is diseased and is leaving so as not to burden her with his death, both reader and driver understand his nobility. The reader also understands that his labor in the mines, and only that labor, has brought him to his death. His employing company, however, pretends that it is free from any responsibility.

Hopeless narratives writ large comprise such novels from the early and middle 1930s as Nelson Algren's *Somebody in Boots* (dedicated to "[t]hose innumerable thousands: the homeless boys of America"[17]) and Jack Conroy's *The Disinherited*. Both books are structured as a sequence of stories about male characters who see themselves as unable, frustrated as they are by a system that gives them neither work nor profit. Men as both fathers and sons face responsibilities they have no means of meeting. Some go crazy. Most die of the effects of inhuman labor—whether in mines, mills, or factories, or on farms. Algren's book begins in a Mexican border town (with Part I titled ironically "The Native Son"); the fall of Stub McKay, head of the motherless family, is signaled by his geographic placement. Good Americans are not supposed to live in such bestial, truly uncivilized situations. Filled with racial epithets and sheer despair, Algren's book may be true to the conditions of his down-and-out characters, but it also has its share of socialistic proselytizing.

Conroy's novel is set in the Missouri mines, with the protagonist's college-educated father trying to eke out a living for his family of eleven. Referred to only as "Father," the head of the family despairs ("The mine is a tomb and once the earth gets over you, it's hard to hump up and cast it off. It crushes them all in the end"[18]) even as he voices his culture's belief in education to his young son: "I'm in a deep ravine with no path to the heights again. I must follow my rut to the end. But your life is just beginning. . . . maybe I can send you off to college. Maybe you can be a lawyer or a doctor."[19] Donovan's words strike with sharp irony; he has just taken his older son, a twelve-year-old, into the mine to work with him. That son, as well as a second child, dies from mine injuries early in the book.

The Donovans were never so poor as their fellow miners; they live in their own house, not one owned by the company. But the well-spoken Canadian Donovan sees himself slipping further and further into debt, and he recognizes the symptoms of his "asthma," so to increase his pay he takes on more dangerous work, that of firing shots for the next day's mining. Dead after only a few months on that job, Donovan leaves his struggling wife to do laundry at the stream—hoping their young children could both care for themselves and live on the little food she provides. *The Disinherited* traces the disintegration of this family, its relatives' families, and its community—page after page punctuated with deaths from the mine accidents that were an expected way of life.

When the mine closes and Larry Donovan, the son who was once promised an education, has to leave home to find work, the book becomes more of a picaresque novel—adventures follow the rails, and for a time Larry works for the railroad—but the structure of each episode is similar: hard work, poverty, unkindness, an occasional misguided attempt from those who have means to help the starving worker class. Even the promise of unionization is soon qualified with disillusionment about how unions too misuse the workers.

Larry Donovan's odyssey is that of anyone who believes in the American dream. While he works as a mechanic, he sends money home to his mother and takes correspondence courses in his few free hours: "I had finished one correspondence course and was on another. When I finished it, I would be an expert accountant. The school's prospectus had assured me that employers would bid avidly for my services then. There would be a cozy bungalow. I'd sit smoking my pipe, a baby or two at my knee, wife leaning lovingly over my shoulders. I'd be looking proudly at my bank book."[20] Yet just years later, long out of work (and what work he had had was dangerous auto industry and high altitude steel work), desperate himself, Larry returns to the Monkey Nest mine site to find his family. His mother and young aunt, with all her children, have taken shelter in the former bar, dishes and pans catching the rain that comes through the roof, eating weeds from along the tracks:

> As I looked closely at Mother and Aunt Jessie, I realized with a pang that time does not wait, and that it is especially relentless with the women of the poor. Aunt Jessie greeted us with a forlorn and toothless grin; her hair that had been so thick and wavy hung on her head in sparse grey strands. Mother had withered away like an apple bitten by the frost; innumerable wrinkles checked her face and converged upon her mouth and eyes.[21]

Arthritic and crippled, his mother walks with a cane made from an old broom.

Restoring the family means crossing class lines. The wealthy farm family that had snubbed the Donovans at the book's start now relies on the miners to save their farm from the bank. The remaining Donovans go to live with the Haskinses on that farm, and Larry goes north with his auto-line friends, convinced that unionization is the only answer. The four men who drive into the cold wind at the end of the book are poised to enact the kind of narrative that would dominate middle-thirties fiction, that of purposeful action meant to unseat the powerful industrial class that made its money from abusing workers. *The Disinherited* stops short of that theme, however, and leaves the reader with only the panorama of human waste and death: mining territory or industrialized landscape, both terrains barren and inhuman.

One of the most interesting writers of the mid-1930s, and one whose fame was as short-lived as his health (because of his own work-induced illness, tuberculosis), was Tom Kromer. Well aware of the lives of mine workers, kept by poverty from finishing his degree at the University of West Virginia, Kromer wrote a novel aptly titled *Waiting for Nothing*, which Alfred A. Knopf published in 1935. Gone is the optimism of writers who think the tragedy of the Depression is the fall of the middle class or the frustration of people trying to rise into that class; Kromer's book is about life among the hoboes and drifters. Originally titled *Three Hots and a Flop*, his novel draws on his two years as a hobo; what is remarkable is that its tight diction and relentless pace makes its narrative seem less oppressive than Conroy's.

As its original title suggests, Kromer's novel is built almost entirely around episodes of hunger. So starved that he is driven to plan robbery, as well as the begging ("dinging") that is his perpetual way of life, the protagonist in this first-person fiction explains rarely, and then in sentences as short as his pseudo-macho statements:

> I have lost my nerve. I walk until I am on the main stem. Never have I been so hungry. I have got to get me something to eat. I pass a restaurant. In the window is a roast chicken. It is brown and fat. It squats in a silver platter. The platter is filled with gravy. The gravy is thick and brown. It drips over the side, slow. I stand there and watch it drip. Underneath it the sign says: "All you can eat for fifty cents." I lick my lips.[22]

There is a comic undercurrent to Kromer's fiction. As the man moves closer to the window, he focuses in on a well-dressed couple who are eating the advertised chicken: "I stare in at the window. Maybe they will know a hungry man when they see him. Maybe this guy will be willing to shell out a couple of nickels to a hungry stiff." Angry that they are only "nibbling . . . they are not even hungry," the protagonist continues his monologue: "I am starved. That chicken was meant for a hungry man. I watch them as they cut it into tiny bits. I watch their forks as they carry them to their mouths."[23]

Each segment of the novel recounts a different episode, but the net effect is a tapestry of hunger: always without adequate work, always hungry, the narrator can see no end to the misery that surrounds him. *Waiting for Nothing* is filled with cryptic narratives of men stealing food (and risking their lives to do so), women leaving infants on benches so that they can be sheltered and cared for, boys jumping trains—dying with injuries—and many deaths. His static plot emphasizes the book's theme: there is no reason to hope. Why write a narrative with a chronology when for these despairing lives, time doesn't matter. A man is as hungry today as he was yesterday—and as he will be tomorrow.

And so is a woman. Kromer's women in soup lines are pathetic, and moving, stereotypes:

I look at their . . . deep eyes. They are sunk in deep hollows. The hollows are rimmed with black. Their brows are wrinkled and lined from worry. They are stoop-shouldered and flat-chested. They have a look on their face. I have seen that look on the faces of dogs when they have been whipped with a stick. They hold babies in their arms, and the babies are crying. They are always crying. . . . because they are hungry.[24]

Strangely without gender, his characters fill an abstracted landscape of city street, lonely train station, bleak farmhouse.

The novel ends with an ambulance called to another mission flop-house, this time to retrieve the body of a nameless man who has died, alone, on a cot, covered with a thin blanket. In its structure as in its powerful yet undifferentiated characters, *Waiting for Nothing* underscores its very theme. And in case the reader has missed that implicit sorrow, Kromer has his protagonist meditate as he waits for the ambulance, "I try to think back over the years that I have lived. But I cannot think of years any more. I can think only of the drags I have rode, of the bulls that have sapped up on me, and the mission slop I have swilled. . . . whatever is gone before is gone. . . . My life is spent before it is started."[25]

Kromer also wrote, probably in response to reviewing a 1935 novel by Edward Anderson he disliked, a short story with that book's title, "Hungry Men." In three parts, dating from 1930 to 1934, the story echoes the bleak outlook for men (regardless of their education), caught as they are in the workless culture of the Depression. Its fragments, too, are connected by stories of food. The opening vignette describes men in Los Angeles eating "lima beans that smell like scorched hair and a stale hunk of bread," rendered with comic dialogue:

We go after the bread and the beans. This hunchback across the table from me fishes this piece of meat out of his beans with his spoon. It is two inches long and has black fuzz all over it. It is not often you get a piece of meat two inches long in the missions, black fuzz or not. It is the leg of an animal and the foot is still on it with the spreaded toes.
"Why in hell don't they skin the seasonin'?" this stiff says.
"Rabbit?" I says. "I see a black rabbit once. Squirrel, maybe . . . "
"Rabbit or squirrel, they oughta cut the feet off the seasonin'," he says.
We gulp down our beans.[26]

Later discoveries in other bowls help the bemused men discover
that the mystery meat is that of a rat. More comic dialogue; the
vignette ends with Kromer's understatement: "we go back to our
beans and eat them and go up and beg for seconds on the scorched
lima beans."[27] Twisting the common understanding of "realism" to
serve his own bitter ends, Kromer presents bleak scene, harsh (and
sometimes kindly) dialogue, and an intentionally unsurprising ending in these fictions of the 1930s. What could be a plausible narrative
outcome when the culture, and the country, was utterly devastated?

The Fiction of Work

Literary critics termed both Conroy and Kromer "apolitical," and
that adjective could be used to describe a number of 1930s novels
that focus on work. While readers have subsequently been trained
to think that all fiction about industrialization, strikes, and unions
must be political in a socialist sense if not a Communist, such works
can also be seen as reflections of the culture's interest in people's
well-being. If people were intent on finding secure jobs that paid
well, if work was the only route to security for both self and family,
then a fascination with the process of finding and keeping a job was
a natural subject for 1930s fiction. The politics of getting a job
(whom one knew, how class and racial lines were followed, the typical unfairness displayed in a tight job market) play a greater role in
the fiction of work than do the move to unification, strike activity,
and outright anticapitalist propaganda.

Nonfiction journalism, too, focused on the kind and condition of
work as a metaphor for what was happening to the promise of
America. When Theodore Dreiser went to observe and write about
the Harlan County miners in 1931, his accounts emphasized that
such working conditions made a travesty of the American dream. So
long as American individualism is the basis of that dream, society
could not become a jungle: Dreiser insists that people have to help
each other, respect each other. True community has to exist to
counter men's animalistic tendency to exploit others.

The cries of the jungle today are no more and no worse than the cries of
the miners in Harlan, or of the cotton mill workers of Gastonia, or the textile
workers of Lawrence, or the agricultural workers of Imperial Valley, or of
the masses in general.[28]

Dreiser's strident complaint is that all these workers are "economic victims of these giant corporations, still posing as individuals, although armed to the teeth with purchased laws, hired officials, and over-awed or controlled courts . . . their dead are everywhere, defeated and starved."[29]

Ranting against big (and inhumane) business became the correct voice for liberal journalists of the decade. Literary critic Edmund Wilson also spent months traveling the country to investigate the corruption of the wealthy. From his time in Detroit, observing the Ford plant and its owner, Wilson wrote essays that were heavily ethnographic: he used the words of Ford plant workers to damn the corporation and the man. "He's a wonder at the publicity, is Ford," said a British worker who had been lured to the States for the company's $5-a-day pay. "Ye get the wages, but ye sell your soul at Ford's,"[30] said another disenchanted employee. When Wilson himself proselytized about what he saw as the demise of capitalism, he concluded that many of the problems at the Ford plant stemmed from the "underlying emotional instability"[31] of "the despot of River Rouge."[32]

Wilson's willingness to villify Ford might have been an easy out; much of the reportage of the 1930s took on the entire capitalist system. Ruth McKenney's *Industrial Valley* (1939) traces labor conflicts and settlements in the rubber plants of Akron, Ohio. Beginning in 1932, her collage of newspaper items reflecting the activities of the town (and such others in the valley as Barberton and Canton) provides background for the continuing narrative of labor conditions. The book builds to the 33 days of the strike at Goodyear Tire and Rubber Company, tragedy narrowly averted time after time, as the C.I.O. (Congress of Industrial Organizations, a prominent alliance of labor unions) finally wins community support and bests the Goodyear management. As McKenney says in her afterword, "Akron set the pattern for industrial America. The rubberworkers were the first to fight their way to freedom."[33] Loosely organized through an intermittent focus on southern rubber workers Job Hendrick and Tom Gettling (fictitious names are used to protect the men and their families), the narrative pulls from a variety of information—economic, cultural, and personal—to make the account both factual and dramatic. McKenney uses dialogue among characters and descriptions of scenes at the plant, on the picket line, and in the workers' homes to create her compelling story. Reading *Industrial Valley* is a great deal like reading fiction.

Some of the most effective writing of the decade depicts the truly inhumane working conditions in the "new" factories. Robert Cantwell took on the lumber industry; Albert Halper's *The Chute* describes a Chicago mail-order plant; many other writers continued criticizing the dangerous, and poorly paying, textile plants. In the manner of the 1930s fiction that presents the fact of hunger with little editorializing, these novels present the fact of inhuman working conditions, the fear of losing jobs, and such unfair labor practices as the speedup and the wage cut. As people were forced to do more and more work for less money, anger surged behind the complacent face of American labor.

Cantwell's 1934 *The Land of Plenty* has as epigraph statistics from the Census of Manufactures, reporting that production of timber products and lumber fell more than 65% between 1929 and 1931. The novel itself narrates the mismanagement of one such factory as men distant from actual labor take over plant leadership. The story is set during the few hours of a night shift when the plant (and half the town) loses power. Despite the suspicions of Carl, the paranoid plant manager and efficiency expert, the outage is accidental, in no way connected with the workers' anger about having to work on a holiday. Plunged into darkness, the workers use that cover to insult—and finally, to attack—Carl, who puts production over all human considerations.

As in some other 1930s novels about industry, *The Land of Plenty* shows a laboring class that is largely unaware of the power of unionization, or even of collective action. Cantwell's structure, in fact, individualizes the characters so that thinking of them collectively is difficult: he uses named narrative sections so that even the villains of the plot (Carl and his spineless assistant, Morley) are given a narrative voice. More important than the management are the laborers: the Native American whose wife is dying (Ed Winters, known as "half breed"), the unscrupulous collegian who cannot afford to return to school (Walt Connor), the kiln man (Frank Dwyer), the crippled fireman (Mike), the oldest employee (Hagen), and his son (Johnny), the youngest of the workers. Hagen is the powerful employee, the man MacMahon, the plant owner, trusts. Yet because he speaks up to Carl, Hagen puts his job in jeopardy.

Cantwell shows plainly in *The Land of Plenty* that men's behavior depends on financial need. As Hagen says apologetically about Johnny's having to work in the plant, "'A year ago I figured I'd have him in school. Now I got my daughter and her two kids living with me. Now we got word my oldest daughter's husband's out of work.'"[34] Rather than supporting his young son in his education, Hagen has to look to the boy for income to support the rest of the family. By contrasting the simple hours-long power outage with the impenetrable malaise of Depression economics, Cantwell uses the microcosm of one shift in a lumber mill to explore human relationships torn apart by financial stress.

The death that occurs early in the novel, which the author suggests is a metaphor for the dehumanization of workers in industry, is that of a new man, nameless for most of the story, crushed under "a large log, six feet through and nine feet long, the butt log of an enormous fir"[35] when the hoist lifting the log suddenly stops. Because the man worked alone in a remote part of the factory, no one found him—"jammed against the piling"[36]—for hours.

A more crucial death or incipient death is that of Hagen, struck at the end of the novel by a police bullet, at Carl's direction. Hagen's victimization makes Cantwell's point in the second half of the novel. Subtitled "The Education of a Worker," Part II of the book focuses on Johnny Hagen as he learns his rights as a laborer. They are very few. First, he is patronized for his age and inexperience; then he is stigmatized because of his father's power. More centrally, he is duped by the college man Walt Connor and made a part of Walt's scheme to rape the factory workers Marie and Ellen Turner (Walt refers to them as "chippies," "bitches," and "little Polacks," reinforcing the prejudice visible in attitudes toward women and ethnic minorities).[37]

While this sexual narrative takes attention away from the factory conflict, a situation which soon escalates into Carl's calling for police support, it reinforces Cantwell's aim to scrutinize class differences. Johnny's father may have intended that he go to college, but clearly Johnny will never be anything but a laborer. Ineffectual as MacMahon is, he still owns—and controls—the factory. Narrative sections told from the point of view of MacMahon's daughter, Rose, make clear her class ambitions and her attitudes toward the workers in the plant. (Other narratives are written from the perspectives of Marie Turner, Winters, Walt, Hagen, and Johnny himself.)

The juxtaposition of these points of view makes vivid the distance between country club life and the workers' existence. As the novel ends, even though the outcome of Hagen's being shot is unclear, other men—identified only as laborers—are described as running for their lives after the police rout:

a dark figure dropped down on a tangle of driftwood. He was a worker; Johnny could see his torn shirt and his loose coveralls. He looked around indecisively before he sat down on one of the logs.
"Another one. . . . "
. . . he was terribly beaten on the face and head. His hair was matted with blood from a cut on his scalp and his eyes were almost closed from the welts on his swollen cheeks. He said nothing as they approached, only holding himself with an inflexible, automatic alarm, ready to run again.[38]

There is no real outcome for Cantwell's book. Rather, it ends with questions—about the future of labor, the future of capitalism, the future of humanity in America. In 1932, reviewing a Kay Boyle novel for *The Nation*, he pointed out that America was a country divided: "the diversity of specialized experiences and the absence of unifying traditions have created barriers to communication almost as great as those supplied by the lack of a common language."[39] By drawing Carl's fearful thoughts as he faces a working class he cannot fathom, Cantwell tries to excuse the man's blind turn to force so characteristic of 1930s management. His narrative strategies, however, cannot change the reader's sympathy for the proletariat, particularly the well-intentioned Hagen and the innocent Johnny.

Cantwell's technique of avoiding authorial interpretation by organizing narrative in fragments, letting each story tell itself, was an inheritance of reportage. Handling sympathy effectively was one of the biggest tasks writers of the 1930s faced. Because reader response to social injustice, like hunger, was predictable, writers worried that their texts would lose impact in the common sympathy. (Readers who were less inclined to sympathize with workers and the poor found other kinds of reading material.) A literary self-consciousness about method and technique during the 1930s was no less visible than it had been during high modernism, and—indeed—a number of the stylistic devices 1930s writers drew on were the same. As Cantwell's title suggests, the irony of "The Land of Plenty" was immediately accessible: readers understood the gap between things as they were and things as they were said to be. The writer's deliberate refusal to construct linear, cause-and-effect narratives paralleled beliefs that the modern world was neither orderly nor predictable: randomness was the norm rather than the exception. And like much modernist writing, 1930s fiction was suffused with a realism so acute, in fact, that earlier decades of American realism paled in comparison.

When critic June Howard revisited the concept of realism, she stressed that its stylistic techniques are drawn from the factual, the detailed portraits of people and objects turn-of-the-century American fiction was famous for. The long novels of the 1930s assume many characteristics of what Howard terms a "documentary project," one which "organizes the narrative according to a unity not of action but of topic."[40] Tom Kromer's various stories of hungry people obtaining food coalesced into "novel" comprise one kind of realistic book; Cantwell's focus on the hour-by-hour behavior of workers waiting in the darkened factory is another; but the clearest use of realistic description and structure is that of Albert Halper's 1937 The Chute.

Echoing the style of his earlier The Foundry, Halper forces the reader to assume responsibility for making the narrative work by listing all characters at the front of the book, as if he were writing a play. With fewer descriptions of people to get in the way, the author and the reader can focus more intently on the maw of the open chute that connects the seven floors of the mail-order company building with the ground. Items ordered are collected and shoved into the chute; men who fall into the open mouth are swept away as easily as a package of shirts. Moving at breakneck speed, the order fillers risk their lives daily to meet production schedules that are increased at the boss's whim. This industry, too, is subject to speedup.

The chute is almost a persona in Halper's novel; it dominates the workers' imaginations as much as it does their hourly schedule:

The packages were disappearing into a big black cavity, a hole which was centered in what appeared to be an upright black boiler standing upon its end. Standing rooted, Paul looked at the hollow-shaped object, noting the black sheen of its sides. The huge cylinder, measuring about twenty-five feet in circumference, was bolt-studded, reaching from the ceiling and driven through the floor. There it stood, huge and sinister, its mouth open.[41]

Powerless before the machinations of the factory, the young workers feel their energies, like their ambitions, sucked into the relentless vortex.

The Chute is also about Chicago. Sam Sussman, father of the family central to the narrative, runs an unprofitable tobacco shop in the city. Halper describes Sussman's opening his store, to place the scene within the city experience:

> The dull morning, lightening perceptibly, showed through the scratch-ings a piece of Chicago he was sick and tired of looking at—a small view of hardened dirty city snow, two pairs of shiny car tracks (steely), a lamp post with an old election sign pasted against its face with the command, "Vote for me!" and a large white horse-radish, minus its plumage, which had been dropped unnoticed to the ground by Mrs. Sussman, or by God knows whom. Mr. Sussman peered at the scene and sighed. He was standing in his slightly soiled long white winter underwear, in his old houseslippers, and though it did not make him any warmer, he began scratching his chest.[42]

Like such other novels as James T. Farrell's *Studs Lonigan* trilogy and Richard Wright's *Native Son*, *The Chute* insists that it is an urban (and specifically a Chicago) book. June Howard's study of realism sug-gests that a focus on environment is one of the tactics from journal-ism and sociology that such novelists borrowed: "The portrayal of a place or milieu provides a . . . general and abstract ordering princi-ple."[43] The writer's emphasis on the facts of city life give credibility to the total presentation. From Theodore Dreiser's *Sister Carrie* and Upton Sinclair's *The Jungle* through Nelson Algren's *Never Come Morning*, American novelists could write double-plotted books, giv-ing readers "both the anatomy of a decline and the anatomy of a particular Chicago milieu."[44]

For Paul Sussman, a young would-be architect, the geography of Chicago dwindles to the harried panic of the fifth floor of the Golden Rule Mail Order building, "the bowels of a new world."[45] Kept from apprenticing by both the Depression and anti-Semitism, he takes a job in the industrial "madhouse" to help his family—the Sussmans can no longer exist without income from both Paul and his older sister, Rae. But on the men's clothing floor, where he works, merchandise "was stacked in great piles as high as the water-sprinklers near the ceiling,"[46] and Paul feels even more closed out from the ambitions of his life. Leaving his "frantic" workplace after his first day,

> He trudged along feeling dead and hollow, with flakes of snow hitting his face. At the intersection of the trolley lines he had to wait for the traffic; the light at the corner gleamed red through the snow. Trucks and wagons, choking the street to the curbing, rumbled along, bound for the railroad and freight terminals downtown.

Paul stood patiently in the cold, waiting for the light to change. Finally it flashed green and, feeling colder and more miserable than ever, he began hurrying along the street. The sky above the dark buildings by this time was whirling with flakes.[47]

Victimized by both nature and the city, Paul exists in his choked urban surroundings, a talented and artistic man forced into the space of "factory worker" without his agreement or volition.

The all too predictable narrative of Halper's novel leaves the reader with the uncomplicated pain of understanding. Paul succeeds at the work he hates. He sees that his sister (in the early stages of pregnancy) must get married and that therefore the family will lose Rae's income; when he is finally offered an apprentice job in an architect's office (which pays much less than the mail-order job), he turns the position down. He will eventually marry his Rosanne, who also works at the Golden Rule, and live his life among people caught as he is in an economic trap. For other employees, however, the narrative is substantially different: some lose their jobs; a few are maimed or killed in factory accidents. Alcoholism helps some stand the manic routine. So does cheating on wives. For the most ambitious, like the manager Myerson, when the company finally fails, only death satisfies.

For all the horrors Halper draws of life in the Chicago factory, he does not take the incipient union activity to any kind of fruition. From the beginning of the book, he shows people trying to organize, but the employees remain loyal to the company. For that reason, their being sold-out (with no warning of any kind) after a frantic day of taking inventory comes as the shocking betrayal it is. The setting of Chicago in winter adds to the recognition of what being unemployed will mean, and the 600-page novel ends, as it began, with the tone of jeremiad that Halper's realism effectively creates.

Chicago's snow is preferable to the heat and the humid stench of the South in the several novels that focus on the 1929 Loray textile mill unionization in Gastonia, North Carolina (see Mary Heaton Vorse, *Strike!*, Grace Lumpkin, *To Make My Bread*, and Olive Tilford Dargan, *Call Home the Heart*[48]). Mill conditions there were even more pathetic than those in the North because women and children were the primary workers. Understanding their arduous labors and their poverty was more moving than reading about men's working conditions in parts of the country where standards of living were

higher. Dorothy Myra Page's *Gathering Storm: A Story of the Black Belt*
uses the persona of a grandmother narrator to recount the story of
her family's coming from the Blue Ridge mountains to work in the
North Carolina cotton mills forty years earlier. Voicing matter-of-
fact descriptions of inhuman living conditions in the company
shacks ("yellow dirt road lined with dingy low-crouching
houses"[49]), Old Marge Marlow admits that present times are even
worse than those of the past.

She and her family had known some success. Lured down to the
mill by the false promise of education for their children, the workers
finally struck—and were given the school. Company bookkeeping
kept their children working rather than learning, however, and
Marge's husband quickly "got the lung trouble"[50] and died. By the
time her own children could have left, conditions had worsened so
that everyone had to work for the family's survival. Marge's daughter—"a bent, old woman at forty-two, her mouth pulling down at
the corners, stomach bulging, hands beginning to twitch, and her
voice rasping and short"[51]—is weaker in both body and will than
her mother. As Old Marge tells her attentive grandchild, "What we
gotta do is fight for our rights."[52]

Gathering Storm is a pastiche of various labor settlements throughout the South, ending with accounts of the Riverton and Gastonia
debacles. Page delineates various injustices, including the drama of
mill owners destroying the strikers' store, putting the workers out
of their homes, and forcing them into tent cities. Not only did the
strikes fail, but Ella May Wiggins, the "song woman" of Gastonia
famous for her "ballits," was shot in the chest and killed. This
woman's death figures in all fiction and nonfiction accounts—it was
one thing to beat men on the picket lines, another to destroy women
workers blatantly, leaving their small children to survive as best
they could. It was also unusual for women to be so prominent in
strike activity.[53]

Gathering Storm was published in 1932 by the Cooperative Society
of Foreign Workers in the USSR. Because of its heavily racial plot
(blacks could not join southern unions, so even these assumed liberals continued the race prejudice endemic to the region), the novel at
its best presents aspects of the American labor experience that were
offensive to readers of the world; no American house would publish
the work. Page includes a terrorizing rape (Elbert Haines, son of a
wealthy white household, attacks Martha Morgan, the family's

young black maid, as she walks home, and then kills her to silence her), which leads to retribution by her brother, Jim, who shoots Haines at a Country Club dance. Then further devastating retribution falls on the black community, which is burned to the ground: the Morgan family—father, mother, and two small children—is shot; an uncle is mutilated, lynched, and shot; and Jim finally shoots himself before the posse of 50 white men can take him.

The way Page incorporates this admonitory tale of racism into the novel is through the friendship that has been formed up north between Tom Crenshaw, the grandson of Marge Marlow, and Fred Morgan, Martha's older brother. Working together on the docks, the young men are both union members and union organizers. When Tom returns to North Carolina, Fred asks him to visit his family—but Tom discovers that the Morgans are all dead. A pivotal moment in Tom's education occurs when he and Fred realize that change in the South will be almost impossible. Fred goes to Russia; Tom, active in the I.W.W., watches his sister and her husband try to survive in the dismal South. Page's subtitle, "A Story of the Black Belt," caused some confusion because the book was thought to be a sociologically based study of textile problems. (A sociologist, Page may have been a bit doctrinaire in her fiction; but she was a part of the 1930s aesthetic in that she tried to provide background and cultural information throughout her novels.) Race is a less visible part of the narrative. The catalyst for Tom's becoming truly political, however, and admitting the real problem of his region, is the murder of the Morgan family. Race and class are inextricably connected, and neither can be overlooked.

The Collective Novel

Sometimes called "strike novels," the 1930 fictions about successful strike activity fit better into a category Barbara Foley has named the collective novel.[54] In *Radical Representations: Politics and Form in U.S. Proletarian Fiction, 1929–1942,* her wide-ranging discussion of the texts and philosophies of the 1930s, Foley writes about this and such other novelistic forms as the social novel; her view is that the collective novel is the only genre that originated from the dominant concerns of the 1930s. Rather than being prolegomena for Communist views or propaganda for striking as political action, these works are often laments about the conditions of labor. Within some of these works, it is difficult to find any explicit ideological discussion at all. The collective novel has as protagonist a group rather than an individual. It tries to use the experimental techniques of formal modernism, many of which are "cinematically conceived," to draw the reader fully into the process of reading the work. As part of its experimentation, it may draw on the documentary practice of naming real characters or using newspaper and newsreel headlines and other recognizable icons from popular culture.[55] The aim of collective fiction is to convince the reader that he or she is a part of the fictional world portrayed—or, rather, that the world represented by the author either is real or has much in common with real existence.

The writer's primary aim is to convince the reader that such a world is in need of change—most obviously, political change. Here the more visible persuasive strategies come into play: the depiction of hunger and miserable working conditions leads the reader quickly to demand improvement. Complaint breeds political action. As Richard Pells describes so convincingly, however, even at the height of American dissatisfaction with its capitalistic system, there was little consensus about what change was necessary.[56] A loosely defined Progressivism underlay many intellectuals' responses to the Depression. Calling for the development of a new "national culture, they envisioned not only an artistic renaissance but also a revolution in values and behavior that would extend beyond the elite and the avant-garde to affect the life of the average citizen."[57]

Altruistic and self-improving, critics of the United States during the 1930s were usually far from joining the Communist Party. There was a great chasm between the complaint about people's conditions and any explicit directive about moving toward Communism. Even the Marxists often did not proselytize for CP involvement—and the Formalists, and less well-defined liberals, often maintained their distance from actual political activity. To equate all critical thinking with the positions voiced by *The New Masses*, for example, is to oversimplify radically. As Pells concludes, "Ultimately the creative artists of the 1930s were responding to issues and values that had little to do with parties, politics, or ideology. Pessimistic about revolution, suspicious of collectivism, introspective in mood and approach, often nostalgic for the past, and instinctively conservative in outlook, they followed a different path from the rest of the intellectual community."[58]

Considering the number of novels published during the 1930s and early 1940s, the fact that so few of them show unionization (i.e., the successful strike) as the means to secure justice for the workers is surprising. (Clara Weatherwax's *Marching! Marching!* is an exception.) Among the best-known is John Steinbeck's 1936 *In Dubious Battle*, an anomaly for the young Steinbeck, who had been writing escapist romances. Another important novel is Maltz's *The Underground Stream*, a 1940 exposé of Detroit auto industry corruption; both Maltz and Steinbeck show strike activity as ineffectual. In Josephine Herbst's more introspective *Rope of Gold* (1939), agricultural workers are the focus for the exploration of middle-class lives caught in the economic and ethical dilemmas of the decade.

Marching! Marching!, a study of the Pacific Northwest lumber industry and its pulp mills, illustrates well the collective novel. Winner of the *New Masses* prize for best novel of 1935, the admonitory narrative opens with the death of the young logger Tim when "the main-line sling gave way, freeing the cable; not seeing the cable leap singing and then snap taut as it whipped through sixteen inch timber like butter."[59] As the labor organizer Mario (who is foreign-born and therefore suspect) helps roll the tree trunk off the body, Weatherwax announces,

> Everyone looked.
> At the place where his face and head at the place where it—the top was sliced neatly off, it must have been when the cable sang. They could see the reddish ooze still slowly boiling crawling out, see the crushed body with bone jags sticking out of the slimy shirt.[60]

Distortion in syntax helps the reader feel the viewers' incredulity: *"It's Tim it might have been me not ducking in time."* [61] The thought rises almost as a chorus as the men recognize that faulty equipment at Bayliss Lumber has caused another accident and cost another life. These are conditions that can be changed.

Weatherwax's use of italics for internal voice aids the complexity of the plot (and with it the several protagonists, characteristic of the group focus). Such separate narrative lines as the workers' subsistence living, Mary and Joe's love, Annie's bereavement when Tim dies, Pete in the role of stoolie, prejudice against Filipino workers (prejudice questioned as the author notes, "Maybe part Jap or even Chinese, but just a poor guy"[62]), the retarded man Silly's role in attacking Mario after the organizer receives a warning letter from

"The America for Americans Committee"—complete with swastika—and the concluding violence against many of the workers who strike.

Weatherwax shows the all-too-logical development of nativist political action (i.e., murder) when powerful community leaders decide to use any means in order to preserve their profitable lifestyles. By uniting with white native-born Americans against the threat of job loss through competition from people new to the skilled labor market—blacks from the South, immigrants, Reds, and women—such "America for Americans" groups justified not only the murder of labor organizers but also the inhuman conditions and poor wages that the working class endured.

In *Marching! Marching!* one of the labor leaders in the pulp mill is a woman. As Mary considers her life as factory worker, the author combines interior monologue with reportage. Listening to her boss praise the new stainless steel installations triggers Mary's response:

. . . *Improvements is okeh, but what about us? It's our labor that buys them. Is there a law we got to take wage-cuts instead of what we produce?*

Dollar ninety-two a day (remembrance unwinding faster than the winders in the papermill could spin). In the morning she punched the time-clock, crossed the concrete floors to her machine in the rewind department. . . . passing the paper under the winder and up between the winder drums, wrapping the paper around the core, slipping it over the core shaft and fixing it into position by collars. . . . She worked at top speed, guarding against cuts or squashed hands, trying to keep her clothes out of the rollers, preventing wrinkles or sags by maintaining the proper tension, keeping watch for imperfections and breaks. Paper dust settled onto her hair and clothes, clogging her nose and throat because the fans didn't work so well.

And there were always efficiency experts all over the place pulling the stopwatch on them.[63]

Firmly grounded in the realities of the workers' lives, readers can then view organizing activity as reasonable. Speedups, wage cuts, and sheer harassment become as objectionable to the reader as to the worker.

As the novel builds, Weatherwax alternates among scenes of the workers' lives at home, at work, and at Nick's place—their only relaxation. Her canvas grows more inclusive: the narrative is not only Mario's or Mary and Joe's but that of the entire community of dissatisfied workers.

Once they have all agreed to strike, Weatherwax creates the chapter describing the strike from newspaper clippings, arranged by bold-faced headlines that are nearly all inaccurate, reportage slanted consistently against the workers. Four to a page, the collage of reportage marshals the "facts" of the strike and false accusations—news being the semblance of objectivity—only to dispel the newspaper's facticity in subsequent chapters. The public voice is not to be trusted; it too has been bought. The news the workers trust is what they hear from their friends:

Terse. Rapid. "And then what?" "Yeah, then what happened?" It had been like this in many houses, many places, from the opening day of the trial, continuing through the full week. From the beginning, "Well, we got there pretty early," different workers telling all about it to those who'd come from picket duty or who hadn't been able to crowd into the courtroom. "Well, we got there pretty early. Just after eight," someone had said.[64]

After the trial, Mary's house is raided and she is beaten, perhaps killed, along with many others. The remaining workers march. Met by armed national guard troops who have been ordered to shoot, the militant employees (who now comprise the group hero of the book—Joe and Mario are jailed or hospitalized, and Mary is missing) continue the march. Like the outcome of these more dominant characters, that of the march itself remains untold. The closing image of the book is of Annie (taking Mary's place) giving the signal for the marchers to head out even as the waiting guardsmen affix their bayonets and put on gas masks. As they march, the strikers begin singing, "Hold the fort for we are coming; / Workingmen be strong!"[65] The implication is one of the people's indomitability, of continuance, of a struggle still fueled with conviction.

The picture of organized protest painted by Weatherwax's novel is vastly different from that of John Steinbeck's 1936 *In Dubious Battle*. His first novel about the working class (following quickly on the heels of his less critical 1935 *Tortilla Flat*) announces its ambivalence toward the issues by its title: drawn from John Milton's *Paradise Lost*, the phrase refers to man's internal struggle, the self-hate that—Steinbeck suggests—marks some malcontents. Accordingly Jim, the out-of-work protagonist, is introduced as a person filled with hatred; the fact that he has reason to dislike capitalism is understated. When Jim asks the Communist strike organizer Harry Nilson, "Did you ever work at a job where, when you got enough skill to get a raise in pay, you were fired and a new man put in? Did you ever work in a place where they talked about loyalty to the firm, and loyalty meant spying on the people around you? Hell, I've got nothing to lose," Harry replies surprisingly, "Nothing but hatred."[66]

This metaphor of a man divided by his own personal angst becomes lost in the novel, however. Set in central California, *In Dubious Battle* grew from an actual situation. Steinbeck had been taken to meet two leaders of the Agricultural Workers' Industrial Union (AWIU) who had been arrested for illegal striking activity. Pat Chambers and Caroline Decker had then hid out near Monterey in Seaside, with a young, articulate Okie (Cicil McKiddy). When Steinbeck had listened to their account of the conflict, according to biographer Jay Parini, "he offered to pay them a small amount of money for the rights to their story; it was his intention to write a story in the voice of a Communist labour leader."[67] Once into the tale, however, Steinbeck found that McKiddy's convictions took over the narrative—and his story became Jim's.

Steinbeck had originally envisioned that this would be a nonfiction project, but his agent convinced him that *In Dubious Battle* should be fiction. The life of the novel undercuts the author's original aim to be objective and distant. While he may have wanted to play the young biologist role, observing the social scene as a "chance to test his theories about group behavior in a large-scale setting,"[68] Steinbeck soon left his theories about "phalanx" behavior behind. Like the reader of *In Dubious Battle*, the author too wanted the group of angry, starving fruit pickers to win against the large farming and land-owning interests of central California.

The momentum of the action of planning toward the confrontational strike carries the second half of the book, and its quick and unexpected culmination in the macabre death of the idealistic Jim—his faceless body used to incite the strikers to march against the armed guardsmen—provides a shocking ending to the book. Jim's murder resonates against the politics of the novel so that, rather than encourage collective activity, Steinbeck's novel warns against it.

The pickers are not the only victims. The small landowners like Anderson and his son, Al—whose lunchroom is destroyed as quickly as the possessions of the fruit pickers—cannot hold out against the monopolistic power of the large corporations: what they decide is what will happen. Their brutality in putting down the incipient strike is drawn without flinching. The "old guy Dan" is another victim of the ravages of poverty: as a spokesman for the misused worker throughout the book, Dan adds humor and belligerence even as he dies broken both in body and mind.

Whether or not Steinbeck intended to be sympathetic to the strikers, *In Dubious Battle* is thoroughly so. What happens in the course of the narrative is that the title itself changes meaning. No longer focused on the interior division of materialistically unsuccessful men like Jim, the book absorbs some of the fragile idealism of party members who truly believe in collective action (the novel also balances its portraits by showing the hypocrisy of many of those leaders, those who are as willing to sacrifice the common people as the large landowners are). At its best, the Communist Party tries to be a positive force. But the reality of the times in California mirrors the times in most industrialized sectors of the economy: human dignity and even life will be sacrificed readily for profits and production schedules.

This is the conclusion Albert Maltz comes to as well in *The Underground Stream*, his 1940 novel about the Depression. Subtitled "An Historical Novel of a Moment in the American Winter," the book uses the form of dramatic tragedy as it traces three days in an actual February 1936 auto plant strike. Set in Detroit, Michigan, and acknowledged as being based on those events, the novel provides a relentless account of the way corporate leaders planned the demise of the strikers. By alluding to "the American winter,"[69] Maltz uses the metaphor of the bleak heart of the Depression, equating the hunger of the times with the hunger for some alternative form of government. His novel illustrates that bleakness.

The Underground Stream differs from most 1930s protest fiction in that it portrays the upper-class owners as well as the workers. Maltz's narrative strategy is to balance accounts of the struggle of the laborers (Princey, Betsy, Ben) against depictions of higher-class society. The book accordingly opens at 10:50 P.M. on Saturday, "the night of the annual ball of the Kingston Country Club of Detroit, and the old colonial building stood gleaming with light."[70] When self-made man Jeffry Grebb, personnel director for Jefferson Motors, enters the club, he admits to himself that he hungers for acceptance and that he would do anything to ingratiate himself with the leadership of his factory.

Rootless and rudderless, Grebb becomes the book's antagonist. It is he who tries to seduce his friend's daughter, and it is he who is finally given the job of killing Princey, the employee who is on his way to organizing a successful strike. Nothing bothers Grebb. Against Maltz's drawing of Grebb's heavy-handed villainy, the characterization of the fascist Kellog, leader of the nativist Iron Guard of the Black Legion that existed in Michigan and Ohio during the mid-1930s, is more empathetic. While Grebb behaves like a robot, it is with passion that Kellog urges his masked friends (dressed in the shroud of the Ku Klux Klan, but in black rather than white),

> "We've got to remember America!" Kellog cried. "We've got to remember that the American people are being menaced on every side by niggers and foreigners and Catholics and Communists and every sort of verminous, poisonous scum! The Kosher boys, the Papists and the long-haired comrades have taken over our American White House! They're making the laws, they're running the roost, they're putting their Jew deal over on the American people as the first step toward pure Communism. . . . "[71]

His frenzied appeal that this armed group wipe out what he calls "dictatorship of the most sinister order" occurs in the basement of his posh suburban home, and his plea is answered with aroused replies: "We'll see the kikes in hell first . . . , Down with Catholics and niggers!"[72]

Blind prejudice incited by the fear of losing one's own place in society leads to the waste and eventual death of the organizers. Maltz's is not a complacent or soothing story. What is most frightening about it is that the people with power are shown to be utterly heartless. Maltz shapes the book so that the entire second half of it chronicles the torture Princey undergoes at the hands of his upper-class captors. *The Underground Stream* reminds the reader of Steinbeck's comment as he sent his agent the manuscript of *In Dubious Battle*: "I hardly expect you to like the book. I don't like it. It is terrible . . . a terrible kind of order."[73] When Maltz's novel ends with a coda describing a farm boy finding the body of Princey, his face calm in his execution, that half page of text reminds the reader that pity was never the agenda in the industrial war that strikers had taken on.

While it may be that some readers consider Steinbeck's *The Grapes of Wrath* as a more positive description of strike activity, that book too shows the comparative ineffectuality of collective action. That the Joads remain alive at the end of the novel is no testament to union activity, but rather to their human ingenuity. Readers may be convinced that Tom Joad, following in Jim Casey's footsteps, will assume a mantle of successful leadership; but history provided another set of narratives for most of the California fruit pickers.

Josephine Herbst attempted to write a different story in *Rope of Gold* (1939), the third volume of her 1930s trilogy. In it she analyzes the power of family to confront an erring son who had come to believe that collective action was the only way to remedy farmers' situations during the 1930s. Jonathan Chance, a well-meaning liberal, cannot stand against his comparatively wealthy family's disapproval; and his vacillation eventually mars his relationship with his wife, Victoria. Herbst draws Jonathan as an idealist fascinated with his own intellectualism: "He had been one of the committee to draft the program and, as he read, he was impressed by the language, identifying his own contribution to the total with pride. As he came to the meat of the document, he took a deep breath, fumbled for the last cigarette in the package, lighted it, took a single puff, and holding it in his hand, picked up the paper again."[74]

Herbst's parallel and contrasting story is that of Steve Carson, a young man with a new baby. In the narrative of the sit-down strike with which the book ends, Carson goes through his own process of evaluating conditions, making choices, and choosing to support unionization: "The union. A warm glow rushed over his body under his stiff clothes as if he were looking out at the street again late yesterday afternoon just after the plant shut down."[75]

In her closing scene of the factory workers waiting inside the plant, watching the national guard assemble outside, Herbst uses the technique of indeterminacy: she does not give the reader the results of the action. Instead, her focus is on Steve's thinking process: "The men were thinking of the union, shyly, proudly, with all the loyalty they had. Steve's throat hurt as he thought. . . . He was seeing the fellows from Saginaw with their heads cut open by the company thugs."[76] He is also valorizing his work: "a job, like a brick, at the foundation of a skyscraper. Not a fancy job, just the run of luck that most men had. A job at the bottom where a man had to feel a man if there was to be any sense to the world."[77]

Like Herbst's novel, much of the fiction of the 1930s is absorbed in defining work, value, and the basic principles of economic health. Whether that fiction focuses on the extreme conditions of people's hunger or on the political strategies people used to attempt to wrest control from factory and land owners, it depicts bravery, honesty, and humanity among the citizens of the working class. More than a reductionist socialist or Communist message, the fiction of the 1930s may have been reinscribing a definition of the common person, one who had been—and increasingly came to be seen again as—the backbone of America.

2

Changing Classes

When Gertrude Stein tried to write about the lower classes in her 1909 *Three Lives,* and Eugene O'Neill made the same attempt in *The Hairy Ape* (1922), "writing down" was a kind of exciting literary primitivism. But the real focus of both Stein and O'Neill quickly took over their writing—creating a middle-class America (as Stein did in her monumental, and definitely middle-class, *The Making of Americans* and O'Neill did in *Mourning Becomes Electra*).

For all the apparent innovation of American modernists, Hemingway's characters, for instance, are properly schooled and respectable. They may delight in being bad, but their very Rotarian guilt adds to the piquancy—and unexpectedness—of that badness. F. Scott Fitzgerald ranged among the middle and upper classes drawing his definitive portraits of the socially elite, as did Edith Wharton, Willa Cather, Ellen Glasgow, and others. When John Dos Passos tried to draw characters from lower-class America, as in *Three Soldiers* and *Manhattan Transfer,* readers more likely turned pages to see how he used language and structure; they were seldom responding to the reality of his people. Glenway Wescott, Kay Boyle, James Branch Cabell—being polite and responsible writers themselves—could not be expected to write believably about the so-called dregs of any society.

That class, however, was the stock-in-trade of the 1930s fiction that focused on the problems of work and remuneration. Lower-class characters needed work. Lower-class characters were often different from the intellectuals who wrote fiction, and in that difference lay problems. Could a writer who had not known the difficulties that were his or her subject write effectively about them? Was a writer working from a kind of "trespass vision"[1] able to convince the reader? When Tom Kromer wrote about being a hobo, readers believed him. What happened when Harvard-educated James Agee wrote about living below poverty level in a sharecropper's house in Tennessee?

Reading 1930s fiction, then, is complicated by the fact that for most middle-class readers, comprehending poverty may require more imagination than we have cultivated. Even in the 1990s, as Constance Coiner writes emphatically, current literary study is burdened by an "obfuscation of class as a category of analysis."[2] Because so much writing in the 1930s existed to describe class differences, this contemporary stance of discounting the issue makes understanding fiction about work, poverty, and protest difficult.

The theme that drives James T. Farrell's work—both *Gas-House McGinty* in 1933 and the three volumes of the Studs Lonigan trilogy—is inescapable differences in class. In fact, the content of his novels might be said to be class itself. When Farrell introduces his "successful" protagonist Ambrose J. McGinty as a man with a "blown-out gut," "convict haircut," and "fatty, but still muscular, neck,"[3] he takes on reader assumptions about heroes. Sitting at a saloon bar, Gas-House has just spit and "missed the spittoon."[4] Cramming the free lunch down hurriedly, McGinty muses on the grief his job—dispatching express trucks, i.e. gas cars—causes him; his silent monologue is peppered with "Goddamn'em!" "Christ!" "Hell . . . them bastards."[5] Hardly the suave and well-born protagonist, McGinty speaks a crude language designed to offend Farrell's readers. "I don't trust them bastards none,"[6] he says later of the men who work for him.

Profanity, bad grammar, and a terse poverty of introspection combine to mark McGinty as a certain type of working-class person. Farrell adds to the mix his epithets about "Jews," "garlic-eatin' spaghetti guzzlers," "Bohunks," and "goddamn Mexs." To McGinty, women are "janes"; as a prostitute approaches him, he thinks "Goddamn hag! Two-bit whore with enough clap and syphilis to infect the whole Japanese army"[7]—ethnic, sexual, and profane insults melded into one.

Only a few pages into the novel, the reader may find it already difficult to identify with Gas-House. Farrell's description assaults the reader. Ignorance is less McGinty's problem than is prejudice, hypocrisy, and sexism. Yet Farrell makes all his stylistic choices work for him, and we begin to understand the gruff yet sometimes fearful Gas-House. In a two-page dream sequence, for example, Farrell shows his protagonist feigning sleep rather than confronting an imagined burglar, and meditating on the noise of cats squalling beneath his window ("A lion reared up in a Douanier-Rousseau jungle"[8]), Farrell uses McGinty's dream life to make him the hero of the conflict. It is in this scene too that the tough Gas-House gently and softly kisses his wife's nightgowned shoulder as she sleeps.

In the early 1930s, the setting of a contemporary book's opening scene in a saloon, calling attention to the men's illegal lunchtime drinking, would have inflamed a conservative reader. Farrell succeeds in creating an objectionable world, an objectionable character, and an objectionable plot—all by writing realistically about a lower-class urban man. Farrell's language challenges reader expectations about what literature is and what language should be used in writing. Hearing the aggressive vernacular of the Chicago streets is less bothersome than seeing the language on the page. McGinty's later developing "piles," worrying over a speech he must give, and eventually being replaced at work constitutes much of the novel's plot. Rather than being McGinty's individual story, however, the work is a mélange of voices—those of men at work, in the saloon, and on the street, repetitively insulting, discussing, and gossiping as they live from day to day.

When the first volume of the Lonigan trilogy, *Young Lonigan*, was published in 1932, fellow writers rushed to defend Farrell's new realism. Poet Horace Gregory, reviewing the novel for *The Nation*, pointed out that "[t]he book is innocent" and that Farrell wrote "honest, unspectacular realism."[9] He mentioned that while the novel had been advertised "for doctors only"[10]—a way of avoiding the Comstock laws and warning readers of Farrell's impolite language—such a precaution was ridiculous. Aside from Farrell's language and the explicit sexual situations of the Lonigan chronicle, the opportunistic sentiments of the character were probably offensive to many readers. By 1934, the publication year of the second volume, while continuing to use his collage pattern of random urban voices, Farrell had begun to focus more expressly on Studs's various acquisitions—of jobs, friends, and sex partners. *The Young Manhood of Studs Lonigan* closes with Studs's rape of an acquaintance. Set amid fragments of speech of other men and women at the New Year's party, this act passes almost unnoticed—it seems to be yet another example of Studs's crude language and overt sexual threat. But in this case, the threat is enacted. Studs tackles Irene as she runs to escape, throws her to the floor (" 'Will you come across now,' he said"), gags her, twists her arm, "gave her an uppercut," attacks her (saying simultaneously, "I won't hurt you. For Christ sake, cut out the stalling"), knees her in the stomach, slaps her "viciously," punches her, and "carried her unconscious to the bed."[11]

When the police arrive the next morning, "Her face was black and blue, and her coat thrown over her torn dress. She winced with each step, sobbed hysterically, shook all over."[12] Questioned by the officer, Studs responds that the nameless "she ain't got no kick. She only got that much!"[13] His crudity brings the book to its close, all but for a half-page coda. Here a black man rolls the drunken Studs (dressed in a suit and coat that were "bloody, dirty, odorous with vomit"[14]), takes the eight dollars he finds, and leaves him to sleep off his party. Studs too, like Gas-House McGinty, is dreaming, thinking that "some day, he would grow up to be strong, and tough, and the real stuff."[15]

Farrell's ironic deflation of Studs Lonigan, which continues in the third book of the trilogy, may have been enough justification for one of the most brutal (if understated) rapes in American fiction; but readers may have stopped following the chronicles. Barbara Foley is right when she states that it is Danny O'Neill, not Studs, who breaks away from "the intellectual sterility and political impoverishment of their South Side neighborhood," while Studs "vents his alienation in racist, antisocial, and self-destructive practices; he eventually dies an alcoholic."[16] Foley links Farrell's Lonigan trilogy with the work Richard Wright does in *Native Son*, in which Bigger's combination of alienation and political ignorance "lead him to admire Hitler and Mussolini and to gain a sense of self through murdering first Mary Dalton and then Bessie Mears."[17]

Changes in Styles of Writing about the Poor

It is at least in part this focus on lower-class characters in a depressingly realistic milieu that separates much 1930s fiction from modernist fiction. When a lower-class character is treated nostalgically—through placement in a pastoral setting, for example (e.g., the titular character of *My Antonia*, by Willa Cather, or Dorinda Oakley in Ellen Glasgow's *Barren Ground*)—a marginal standard of living is acceptable, even ennobling. Similarly, in Ruth Suckow's *The Folks* (1934), the saga of the inevitably poor Ferguson and Luers families holds the same kind of interest as an Alger narrative: readers are assured that prosperity would follow good, moral behavior. Suckow shows Ferguson thinking to himself after he and his wife return from a long-awaited trip to California, "They had their home to come back to—some folks, when it came to the end, didn't even have that much. Folks as good as *they* were."[18] In effect, such moral behavior underlies Janie's rewards in Zora Neale Hurston's *Their Eyes Were Watching God* (1937)—her great love for Tea Cake, followed by her return home to a good friend and her acknowledgment of her satisfaction with herself and her life choices.

Henry Roth's *Call It Sleep*, another 1934 book, also works with the inescapable poverty to be found in "the Golden Land" by such immigrants as the Yiddish-speaking Schearl family: "here in the new land is the same old poverty,"[19] the observant wife says sadly. Some semblance of family unity might come with the child David's near-death, but the stresses of New York ghetto life have already destroyed much of the Schearl stability. In like fashion, Richard Wright's characters in his 1930s stories, including the novellas that comprise the 1938 *Uncle Tom's Children*, are mostly innocent and trusting blacks. Crippled by inarticulate speech, they yet make themselves understood. In Wright's view at that time, their poverty and forced exclusion from mainstream life because of race had not deadened their moral responses. By the time he wrote *Native Son* (1940), however, Wright had decided that the softly apologetic tactic of making blacks understandable in their changing sociological context was ameliorating the effects he wanted his writing to have. *Native Son* is an assaultive, shocking study—intentionally disruptive to white complacency.

James T. Farrell brought to his depiction of the Studs Lonigan style of character a similarly unsympathetic speech and behavior. Studs, wearing his bellicose and sexually aggressive name, is hard to redeem from what might have been considered the natural effects of South Side Chicago life. To continue the narrative through three long volumes was expecting readers to follow Lonigan's odyssey of vulgarity with an anticipation that the plotline denied, however. What may have passed for humor or innovation—the character's brusque responses to other people, his sexist and racist behavior—could not sustain a trilogy.

When John Dos Passos planned *U.S.A.*, his three-volume collage of America, he chose a more varied, more palatable set of characters, ranging from the wealthy to the down-and-out. Women's lives were also portrayed, often—at least in the case of Mary French—in more detail than the men's. Advertised as a novel about the proletariat, Dos Passos's only worker character, Mac, actually disappears in the second and third books; he serves to introduce the 1930s issues in *The 42nd Parallel,* when his history as the boy Fenian McCreary (Fainy) takes up the first fifth of the book. On the run from Chicago and a crooked employer, Fainy meets a young hobo socialist, discusses Bellamy's *Looking Backward* with him, and becomes "Mac." Their dialogue—"It's the workers who create wealth and they ought to have it instead of a lot of drones"[20]—echoes the starting point of Fainy's family narrative, when his father complains to his uncle, "So long as I've lived, Tim, I've tried to do the right thing. . . . I've been a quiet and respectable man, steady and misfortunate ever since I married and settled down."[21] Sold-out and unable to pay his wife's funeral expenses, the older McCreary runs away to Chicago in search of work. The all-too-familiar story of men without hope gives the first novel of Dos Passos's trilogy an appeal which his later volumes, *1919* and *The Big Money,* their attention turned to more prosperous characters, relinquish.

Technique saved the *U.S.A.* trilogy for a time; it was considered a miracle of avant-garde craft. By allowing for the various kinds of narrative structure, Dos Passos gives a reassuringly predictable signal to modernist readers: the blocked, long-line prose poems describe such historical figures as Eugene Debs and Woodrow Wilson; the headline and newsreel sections are visibly self-descriptive. Farrell, too, sometimes created an amalgam of other characters' voices surrounding Lonigan, but there was no format change to signal readers that point of view was different.

Class and Genre Fiction

There is another consideration in determining why neither the Farrell nor the Dos Passos trilogies are read much today. Fiction readers of the early 1930s had been increasingly wooed away from serious, social-issues fiction by a relatively new genre, the mystery and detective novel. As uncouth in language and social attitudes as Studs Lonigan, many of these new American heroes were as titillating in their sexual exploits (which included large-scale mistreatment of women) as they were ingenious in their sleuthing.

William Marling calls this "dark style of narrative"—which also draws on contemporary happenings in film, economic change, and technological surfeit—"the American Roman Noir" and traces it to the writers' inevitable guilty reaction as the Depression followed the magical prosperity of the 1920s.[22] Sexual excess was a corollary to the financial excesses that had marked the modern years, and any narrative that could incorporate more sexual relationships (described matter-of-factly rather than obliquely) would hold the readers' interest. So in *The Maltese Falcon* (1930), Dashiell Hammett's Sam Spade is surrounded by his beautiful office assistant, Effie Perine; Brigid O'Shaughnessy, an even more beautiful client (who is herself a killer); and Iva Archer, wife of his now-dead partner, with whom he has had an affair. Every time Spade's office door closes, the reader is alerted to possible romantic (or at least sexual) adventures.

That Spade gives Brigid over to the police to serve time for her murders bears out what Marling considers the primary appeal of the new detective genre. Despite his sexual longing for her, Spade is still a man of honor: Brigid must pay the price for her killings. As Marling states it, "desire must serve economic ends."[23] In the climactic scene, when Spade confronts Brigid with her murders and her duplicity, she pleads for his love—and her freedom. Admitting that he does love her, Sam sets the tone for what was to become the classic "tough guy" pose as he assures her,

" . . . if you get a good break you'll be out of San Quentin in twenty years and you can come back to me then. . . . I hope to Christ they don't hang you, precious, by that sweet neck." He slid his hands up to caress her throat.[24]

The dichotomy of his ruthless words combined with his gesture of lovemaking shaped the image of the businessman sleuth, whose work came before his emotional loyalties.

Hammett's detective novels (first published serially in *Black Mask* and then in book form between 1929 and 1931) gave the literary world a genre compatible with the Western. Written about men, for men, and by men, the detective novel assumed that its readers agreed with its moral stance. In *The Maltese Falcon*, Spade's sending Brigid up is justified because she has killed his business partner. (No matter that Spade himself disliked the man and was cuckolding him.) Lonely in a world governed by the materialistic and the rational, these 1930s protagonists considered themselves morally superior to a culture that was growing increasingly corrupt. That they often worked outside the legal system, as symbolized by their distance from the police, was an index of their outsider status. As the ravages of Depression poverty cut further and further into the fabric of normal life, few people lived lives beyond suspicion.

Financial gain is the driving force for Brigid's murders as she struggles to acquire the valuable maltese falcon. In James M. Cain's 1934 *The Postman Always Rings Twice*, Nick Papadakis's insurance is the apparent motivation for his murder by his wife, Cora, and her tramp lover, Frank Chambers. Borrowing the stylistic qualities of the detective genre for use in a plot that needs no unraveling (the crime and its aftermath are the narrative), Cain opens the story of the death of the small garage-restaurant owner, a Greek who is himself an outsider, with an understated but passionate sex scene only seven pages into the book.

> Somebody was out front, rattling the door. "Sounds like somebody trying to get in."
> "Is the door locked, Frank?"
> "I must have locked it."
> She looked at me, and got pale. She went to the swinging door, and peeped through. Then she went into the lunchroom, but in a minute she was back.
> "They went away."
> "I don't know why I locked it."
> "I forgot to unlock it."
> She started for the lunchroom again, but I stopped her. "Let's—leave it locked."
> "Nobody can get in if it's locked. I got some cooking to do. I'll wash up this plate."
> I took her in my arms and mashed my mouth up against hers . . . "Bite me! Bite me!"
> I bit her. I sunk my teeth into her lips so deep I could feel the blood spurt into my mouth. It was running down her neck when I carried her upstairs.[25]

The terse and almost meaningless dialogue (what is the significance of playing this game with the locked door?), the stark sentence syntax, and the weirdly sensational blood-letting in the culmination of the scene are all marks of the highly-charged simplicity that Hemingway and other "realistic" writers of the times had used. Cain's narrative is an almost entirely sexual one, replete with the animalism of the two young and very white Americans. Ethnic prejudice spills into the plot, as Frank and Cora justify her husband's murder without much of a qualm. Referring to Nick as "the Greek," Frank lets himself be co-opted by Cora's American dream of money and position. As she tells him early in the novel, "it won't do, Frank. That road, it don't lead anywhere but to the hash house. . . . I want to work and be something, that's all. But you can't do it without love. . . . Anyway, a woman can't."[26]

Cain transfers the cold objectivity of a Sam Spade to Cora, a woman who uses the physical passion of "love" to further her own ends. Focusing on her rather than on Frank, Cain continues the emphasis Hammett had initiated when he created Brigid. No longer simply a helpmeet, a woman of the 1930s had the capacity, and the ambition, to kill on her own; she was not above furthering her own dreams at the expense of her man's. The stereotype of women in fiction was changing with the times.

In Cain's narration, however, Cora remains the love object. "Rip me! Rip me!"[27] constitutes much of her lovemaking dialogue; and her torn clothes and black eye at the murder scene are repeated later in the text. As the plot winds into a labyrinth of crooked lawyers and their accomplices, making money regardless of innocence or guilt, the reader becomes as disgusted with the culture as with Cora and Frank.

The denouement of *The Postman Always Rings Twice* undercuts any radically new view of woman. Pregnant with Frank's child, Cora marries him; later in the day, she becomes ill while they are swimming. When he drives her to the hospital and tries to pass a car, he hits a cement culvert. She is killed instantly.

According to the lawyers who had tried them for Nick's murder, Frank enacted the profit motive again: now married to Cora, he inherits all her money. Convicted as much for the original murder as for Cora's death, Frank awaits execution at the book's end—a surprisingly moralistic ending for a tough crime novel.

Drawing once more on the 1927 Ruth Snyder–Henry Judd Gray murder case that was the starting point for *The Postman Always Rings Twice*, Cain in 1936 published another insurance scam story, *Double Indemnity*. Because they could collect double the premium on a policy if the holder died on a railroad journey (hence the title of the book), Phyllis Nirdlinger and Walter Huff murder her husband and plant his body on a train. Huff, an insurance salesman, is both more prosperous and more moral than Chambers had been—and this reinscription of the wife-and-lover-kill-husband plot has deeper psychological overtones. Phyllis, her voice "hard as glass,"[28] continues to be the manipulator, evincing an erotic excitement at "the moment of audacity that has to be the part of any successful murder."[29] Huff comes to a defeating realization, as he recounts:

> I stared into the darkness some more that night. I had killed a man, for money and a woman. I didn't have the money and I didn't have the woman. The woman was a killer, out-and-out, and she had made a fool of me. She had used me for a cat's paw so she could have another man, and she had enough on me to hang me higher than a kite.[30]

Mesmerized by Phyllis after he relinquishes hope of loving another, Huff agrees to a suicide pact with her from on-board ship. Despite her money, Phyllis had told him, "There's nothing ahead of us."[31] Once more in charge of their lives, she orchestrates their jump by moonlight into the shark-infested waters.

By the time oil company executive Raymond Chandler began his publishing career with *The Big Sleep* in 1939, the Roman Noir genre was as well-established as the legitimacy of murder for financial gain. Characters who might seem to be middle-class pair with those of lower origins and seduce and kill for the privilege of becoming (comparatively) wealthy. Using the American dream writ in blood, mystery and detective writers employed a quantity of sexual scenes to lure the reader into assuming that crime must have an emotional justification: its usual justification, however, as the tangled plots unraveled, was financial gain.

In both *The Big Sleep* and *Farewell, My Lovely* (1940), Philip Marlowe takes on enigmatic situations that hinge on a family's maintaining social and economic position. In *The Big Sleep* Marlowe, who is employed by the Sternwoods, an oil family for three generations, finds himself surrounded by the lush life of the rich, although the behaviors of both daughters, Carmen and Vivien, are perplexing. Involved with pornographers and other disreputable men, Carmen is finally discovered to be the victim of a seizure disorder. Unfortunately, she kills when she is in her trance state. As Chandler structures his novel, her physical disability seems to symbolize the corruption of the extremely wealthy. Even though he narrowly escapes death at her hands, Marlowe is hardly proud of his discovery of either her illness or her crimes.

Surrounded by a gallery of more varied grotesques in *Farewell, My Lovely*, the detective here leaves his sanctuary, his inviolable rented room, to search for the mysterious Velma Valento. Married to the wealthy Grayle, leaving behind her poverty and her ethics, Valento uses her sexuality to trap Marlowe. Replete with the sensuous dialogue and lovemaking of a Hammett novel, this work also presents the detective as vulnerable, sometimes clumsy, and sometimes wrong. It also creates a tough-guy humor. Here is Marlowe talking to himself while imprisoned in a locked room:

"Okey, Marlowe," I said between my teeth. "You're a tough guy. Six feet of iron man. One hundred and ninety pounds stripped and with your face washed. Hard muscles and no glass jaw. You can take it. You've been sapped down twice, had your throat choked and been beaten half silly on the jaw with a gun barrel. You've been shot full of hop and kept under it until you're as crazy as two waltzing mice. And what does all that amount to? Routine. Now let's see you do something really tough, like putting your pants on."[32]

Pushing the ironic tone that is common for this genre, Chandler takes a more visibly satiric role in recounting the foibles of his pitiful characters.

Velma is less pitiful than some. Her death, after she first kills the policeman who has tracked her, comes from two bullets through her heart—a supposed impossibility, but an act befitting the cool, ambitious woman. By killing herself, she saves her aged, and still loving, husband from the horror of watching her on trial. Again, Chandler's style echoes that of Hammett and Cain:

"Let's go then," she said and stood up and grabbed up her bag and got her coat from a hanger. She went over to him holding the coat out so he could help her into it. He stood up and held it for her like a gentleman.

She turned and slipped a gun out of her bag and shot him three times through the coat he was holding.[33]

As ruthless in her behavior here as any male protagonist in similar fiction, Velma and women characters like her helped to question the formulaic patterns so common to detective—and other genre—fiction. Like the Western, the detective or crime novel was predicated on the protagonist's failing to adjust to a corrupt society and accepting the loneliness of his or her outsider status with equanimity. Such loneliness is the opposite of the community involvement that most 1930s social-issues novels championed. From these two strains grew the psychologically complex, introspective novel, which became a common kind of fiction during the war years and after.

In more than a few respects, one link between this popular mystery and detective fiction and more serious proletarian fiction is the fast pace of the story. During the 1930s, narrative finally learned to *move.* Much modernist fiction had worried the small detail (either realistic or symbolic), working poem-like to focus the reader's attention on the thing itself. (Sometimes the reader is not sure what the object so emphasized has to do with the story.) Thirties writing, in contrast, grew increasingly less precious. It reached a kind of apex in the later 1930s when the intensity of Chandler's and Cain's storytelling kept readers breathless on the edges of seats (both in libraries and in movie theaters). That reaction was not so different from readers who were experiencing the equally dramatic pace of Maltz's *The Underground Stream,* Steinbeck's *In Dubious Battle,* or Wright's *Native Son.*

Women Writers during the 1930s

For all the sexual importance of women characters in the detective and crime novels (and the films made from them), little attention was paid to women writers who were working seriously during Depression years. Several of the novels now studied as being representative of that writing—Meridel LeSueur's *The Girl** and Tillie Lerner Olsen's *Yonnondio*—were not even published as books until more than 30 years after the period. It is obvious, however, that the writing of women reporters and novelists colored the impressions of the world of readers at large and subtly influenced the work being published by the more visible male authors. As David Minter suggests, "Writing of the thirties bears the marks of 'strangers' and 'outsiders'—Southerners, Jews, blacks, and women—for whom writing was necessarily a way of testing and transgressing boundaries."[34]

With this emphasis on a new composite view (a look at society from the outside edges to the center rather than from an unquestioned, and unquestioning, core) critics have underscored the novelty of the proletarian period per se. At few other times in history have previously unheard, even silenced, voices so dominated the literary landscape. As we have seen, too, these voices often stemmed

*See my Modern American Novel, 1914–1945 for a full discussion of The Girl.

from a class that had frequently been absent from literature—that of the poor, or the uneducated, or both.

Constance Coiner, Barbara Foley, Charlotte Nekola, and Paula Rabinowitz have assessed some of the problems of being a woman writer within a labor-based culture. A great many women did not work outside the home; with a literary aesthetic defined on the basis of being a "worker-writer," few women felt competent, or welcome. As Rabinowitz concludes,

a contradictory relationship developed for the female authors who were engaged in the project of creating a revolutionary aesthetic. As women, they were separated from the sources that were to feed the revolutionary writer: if they were working class, it was unlikely that they had been industrial workers. . . . If they were intellectuals, their class position alienated them from the workers, even if their education better enabled them to create literature. . . . neither literary radicalism nor literary history could fully accommodate radical female voices.[35]

Whether or not women were in the workforce, they still experienced the shocking poverty of the times. Most women could not find jobs, at least not high-paying ones. When they did find work, their low pay added to their husband's equally low income meant continued need. As Winifred D. Wandersee points out, "Over a third of all married women workers were in families in which the husband made less than $600."[36]

We have already seen the importance to the period of Josephine Herbst's family trilogy, especially *Rope of Gold;* the effectiveness of pastiche in both LeSueur's *The Girl* and Ruth McKenney's *Industrial Valley;* and the poignant stridency of Dorothy Myra Page's *Gathering Storm* and Clara Weatherwax's *Marching! Marching!*. Another evocative study of women's lives during these bleak years is Tillie Olsen's *Yonnondio: From the Thirties.* With a frightening view of the open throat of the Wyoming mine, described so vividly from the perspective of six-year-old Mazie Holbrook, Olsen taps into the reader's pervasive fear—for the well-being and safety of the children of the poor. Whereas many of the 1930s novels of hunger and work emphasize the need of entire families, the plight of those families' children more often dominates fiction by women.

In many respects, Mazie is the protagonist of the novel, and Olsen writes lovingly of the bond between her and her mother, Anna. One of her most touching scenes is of an outing during which Anna forgets her constant, deadening worry and wears a "remote, shining look" as she blows dandelion fluff around her children.[37] But there are also scenes of her harsh treatment of the youngsters, when she is pushed beyond human endurance in her search for food, housing, and stability.

The family moves from the Wyoming mine to a Dakota farm to an Omaha slaughterhouse and packinghouse (in the latter area, Mazie's father, Jim, also works in a sewer). The brutalizing working conditions change Jim into an abusive man, even to the point of his raping Anna after she has suffered a miscarriage. In his sometimes lengthy absences from the family, Jim also shows his belief that men's work is superior to women's (he early tells Anna, "Quit your woman's blabbin'"[38]). Olsen presents an all-too-typical family situation, but to ameliorate its tensions, she uses inset narratives that have little to do with the Holbrooks. These interpolations, combined with the distinctive narrative voices that tell the primary story, mark *Yonnondio* as modernist as well as collective.

More lyrical than most of the 1930s realistic fiction, Olsen's novel plays on several strands of reader empathy. In her descriptions of the common poverty, she traces the characters' endurance, as well as nuances of change in their relationships. One of Olsen's narrative techniques is to counterpoint despair with hope. While *Yonnondio* does not end happily, it closes with a scene of the family united, listening to the miracle of the wireless, a scene that suggests promise.

One of the most lyrical 1930s novels is Josephine Johnson's Pulitzer Prize–winning *Now in November*. Unexpectedly dour, the book leaves the reader to cope with the suicide of the oldest daughter, Kerrin; the death of the beloved mother from burns (and her loss of any will to live); the departure of the hired man who might have loved the narrator; and the bankruptcy of the exhausted father and his two remaining daughters. Johnson's poetic style serves to blunt the shock of these events, even while the tragedies accumulate rapidly during the last quarter of the novel.

Beginning with the promise of spring, the book traces the growing season on the heavily mortgaged farm. Although things seem to be going well, specific events turn tragic: a birthday party for the father ends with the slashing and bloody death of the family's beloved dog when Kerrin throws the knife that was her present for her father into the dog's face. Devastated by summer drought, the family farm seems incapable of surviving another year (one of Johnson's most poetic qualities is her refusal to provide an exact chronology—the text moves from one spring to another, from one November to the next. As the narrating daughter, Marget, says, "The years were all alike and blurred into one another"[39]).

Inflected by the farmers' anger that milk prices had fallen, the novel is a strike narrative of sorts. But its focus—in the context of a sense of mystically passing time as the daughters age—remains almost entirely on the family rather than on the farm or the community. And the voice of the responsible Marget gains power without ever accepting any easy answers. As she says near the end of *Now in November:*

> I do not see in our lives any great ebb and flow or rhythm of earth. There is nothing majestic in our living. The earth turns in great movements, but we jerk about on its surface like gnats, our days absorbed and overwhelmed by a mass of little things—that confusion which is our living and which prevents us from being really alive. We grow tired, and our days are broken into a thousand pieces, our years chopped into days and nights, and interrupted. Our hours of life snatched from our years of living.[40]

Watching her father age, recognizing that he will be unable to care for her and her sister Merle, Marget accepts her role: "I saw how the debt would be Merle's and mine to carry by ourselves—how many years I do not know, but for a long and uncounted time. All life perhaps. . . ."[41] In Johnson's tough, almost dry, narrative of a family, nothing is romanticized—not the relationship between father and mother, or that between parents and children, or that among siblings. The strained conditions of life have destroyed nearly all the human understanding and love that they had known in younger years. That, rather than any economic debacle, is the tragedy Johnson draws.

Using a more realistic style, Caroline Slade also focuses on the domestic side of poverty in her ironically titled *The Triumph of Willie Pond* (1940). In this unbearably real narrative, the husband and father—Willie—is absent because he has been sent to a sanatorium for his very advanced tuberculosis. The life of the Pond family, then, is truly the matriarchal scene—mother and children struggling to exist under various welfare plans.

Each narrative recounts a triumph. Willie improves miraculously, despite the grave damage he has done his lungs and his entire body working constantly, frenetically, in the low-paying menial jobs that

Slade chronicles so movingly. After two years of good care, sunlight, exercise, and above all food, he is ready for release from the institution. His return home comes with a warning, however: he cannot overwork, he must continue to have good food and rest, and he must lead a calm life or his tuberculosis will become active once more. What Willie would return to, of course, is the same inhuman condition of working at jobs nobody else will take. Worse, as he and his family already have learned, they cannot exist on the pay he will take home from such labor.

The family narrative also describes the triumph of Sarah and her children once they are better nourished. Slade shows her reader what malnutrition does to every human being: *The Triumph of Willie Pond* is a remarkable book in that it avoids the self-pity that might have accompanied the full detail of what the family ate, how that little food was—or was not—prepared, and how the children responded to "normal" nutrition and a "normal" mother's care. Slade is particularly adept at making Sarah's transformation from a sluggish, unable homemaker to an energetic and loving woman believable. Once the family takes root again, after several months of good care, the Ponds become engaging characters, filled with ability and distinct personalities. Slade insists in her narrative that allowing them to have a better place to live, adequate money for food and clothing, and the independence of managing their own resources— instead of being treated like guilty animals (as they were under a previous welfare system, as administered by Miss Southard)— makes such change possible.

As long as the novel is, it seems economically written. Slade must convince the reader, as she sets out to do in the first quarter of the book, that Willie is working harder—digging ditches for the city— than is humanly possible. She painstakingly describes his trip home each night, walking the blocks of uneven sidewalks, wishing his bug-infested flat were on the first floor. The characters of the children are drawn distinctively—Mary, who will leave home and use her sexuality to live; Betsey, the smart and responsible daughter; George, whose dream is to have his own car (or at least parts for one); Ned, the eleven-year-old; Jackie, the youngest, whose symptoms of malnutrition amuse rather than warn the family; and Phoebe, the baby, wearing the same diaper for hours at a time—the fruits of fourteen pregnancies, and many infant deaths. Pregnant once more, Sarah is to have two more children before the novel ends.

Reaching an impasse of desperation, Sarah and Willie fight repeatedly. As she tells him when they learn that he will be paid only every two weeks, "One meal of rice, and about five prunes apiece. And you don't get your pay for five days yet, and no trust anywhere."[42]

Luckily, when Willie collapses and is found to have tuberculosis, the family moves from one set of welfare rules to another. Without a breadwinner, much more aid is available to them. The two hundred pages that describe their improvements in living, health, education, and behavior are fascinating reading. Slade's finesse as a storyteller makes what could be tedious events, or a lack of event, compelling. Her choice is to end the book abruptly—as the family and Willie himself realize that his returning home, his illness arrested, will mean the end of the family's comparative prosperity. Willie even pushes aside his natural timidity and goes to the welfare offices, and to his physician, for specific information: he knows now that if he returns his family will have to live as they did before his illness, and he cannot face sending them back into that inhuman life. So he kills himself before he is released from the sanatorium. As a widow, Sarah will continue to receive the benefits that make family living possible. The consoling voice of the sanatorium doctor echoes ironically through the ending of the novel: "When you've got your health, you've got everything, Willie."[43]

Slade's highly topical treatment of the welfare system, complete with discussions between a young and an older social worker expressing different philosophical positions, does not detract from the sheer human interest of the novel. *The Triumph of Willie Pond* remains as a remarkably presented family case study, never lacking in narrative interest. Like the Olsen and Johnson works, this book elevates very poor characters into heroism, forcing the reader to accept the obvious humanity of Willie and Sarah, their children, and their neighbors, regardless of their inability to earn adequate livings.

To move from these varied 1930s women's novels that recount the grim lives of the poor to Tess Slesinger's *The Unpossessed* is to change classes dramatically. Slesinger's harshly satiric look at upper-class New York intellectuals (drawn from her intimacy with the leftist *Menorah Journal* group, the journal her husband, Herbert Solow, had cofounded) shows the way the Depression changed even carefully insulated lives. Not that these people are hungry—

no, their self-centered concerns are with what will become of their world as they know it. They convince themselves that in these times they should avoid bringing children into the world—and so, logically, there is little need for marriage. The dominant narrative of the novel is whether or not Margaret will abort the fetus she is carrying.

Tonally, the novel begins with Margaret Banners Flinders's grocery shopping and deciding that even providing food for her puritanical husband, Miles, is futile: "Everything's withering."[44] Losing interest in this pretentious intellectual who wants her to end her pregnancy, Margaret finds herself attracted to the sycophantic Jeffrey. Even though this young magazine editor is married (to a woman who bears the first name and a more than subtle resemblance to Norah Joyce), during the course of the novel he has both flirtations and sexual affairs with several women besides his wife, eventually using his sexual charm to secure funding for his magazine.

Slesinger's 1934 book foreshadows both Djuna Barnes's *Nightwood* and Mary McCarthy's *The Company She Keeps*. A study of the male ego, with scenes of homosexual as well as heterosexual attraction, the book sends up the high-flown rhetoric of both intellectuals and higher-class patrons of the arts. When Dr. Bruno Leonard, teacher and spokesman for what has come to be seen as the ineffectual liberal position, finds that pages of his speech have been torn into bits by the young Emmett, a student in whom he is interested, he delivers a parody of what would have been his liberal monologue. As the professor's student-disciples realize that all Bruno's convictions are sham, they leave him in the midst of the high-society audience, pontificating in ways his older listeners approve. In the changing mélange of the Depression, even the radical Dr. Leonard has succumbed to more convenient beliefs.

Slesinger presents a world where the elite are guilty of deep cynicism, not to mention anti-Semitism and anti-intellectualism. Her title names the advantaged people who are not only "unpossessed" but "uncommitted." Without belief in the value of civilization, these urban characters remain an unsympathetic, vacuous lot. When Margaret agrees to the abortion that Miles has been encouraging her to have throughout the book, the novel ends on a most sterile note. If this is the promise that economic wherewithal can supply, then America is truly in trouble.

The work of women writers, while focused more often on the domestic situation that poverty makes unbearable (particularly in terms of the lives and hungers of children), shows the same range of diverse approaches as the fiction of men during the 1930s. Not paucity of talent, but rather a lack of market demand for women's realistic writing, meant that publishing works by even these skillful artists was difficult. Somehow suspicious that women wrote too sentimentally, too autobiographically, or too personally to achieve the tough surface the collective novel aimed for, editors and publishers overlooked the great pool of ability that could have been theirs.

Literary History, Class, and the Decade Problem

Literary history complicates our reading of these materials, too—whether by male authors or female—because it pretends that it is possible to separate 1930s fiction from that written in the 1940s. Obviously, the concerns of the Depression years had not disappeared by the early 1940s. Most writers take several years to compose novels. John Dos Passos's so-called 1930s trilogy, *U.S.A.*, was written throughout the late 1920s, its first volume (*The 42nd Parallel*) appearing in 1930; its second (*1919*) in 1932; its third (*The Big Money*) in 1936; and—with the publisher's prayer, to increase slim sales—the three-volume composite (now newly titled *U.S.A.*) in 1937. Similarly, James Agee and Walker Evans's photo-text *Let Us Now Praise Famous Men* was published in 1941, though it had been in process for more than five years (the actual photos along with the men's live-in experience on which the text was based coming from the summer of 1936, when the project had been commissioned by *Fortune* magazine).

Caroline Slade's *The Triumph of Willie Pond*, her study of the truly murderous idiosyncrasies of the welfare system, was being written for several years before its publication in 1940. Ernest Hemingway spent more than a few years preparing to write, and then writing, his 1940 best-seller about the Spanish Civil War, *For Whom the Bell Tolls*. His play about that cataclysm, *The Fifth Column*, appeared in 1938; related short stories were published in 1938 and 1939. For Richard Wright, the completion of *Native Son*, published in 1940, was just another marker on his decade-long hegira to become a writer. Immersed in the sociology and political thought of the University of Chicago, reading voraciously in modernist and leftist writing,

Wright saw the possibly immense market for fiction that acknowledged the real problems of being poor and black in the States.

It has become a commonplace of history to note that there was no recovery from the economic chaos of the 1930s until well into World War II. Accurate in its general premise, the statement still obscures the fact that many of the underclass (the new protagonists of much American fiction) never recovered at all. Lost in the welfare system or angrily resistant to that system, hoboes and other drifters were so far removed from any geographic or financial stability that they could not have applied for either work or welfare. Years of living on the run, years of having literally nothing meant that finding decent clothes and shoes, using a razor, and being at a factory gate to apply for work at the right time was impossible. The homeless culture arising in the thirties, which told time by the sun and lived from mulligans cooked over a fire of sticks, was permanently devastated. Ambition, order, control—those pillars of American dream behavior—had been, first, eroded and then erased by a poverty that turned human beings into, simply, beings.

Political alignments also remained unclear. If some writers joined the Communist Party (many of those who at one time or another had professed belief in collective principles never actually joined), they may have resigned quickly. As was typical of much of the fiction written during the 1930s, which often seems apolitical in its philosophy, many writers too focused on individual situations without accepting doctrinaire systems. A number of writers showed their sympathy with the North Carolina workers during the 1929 Gastonia mill strike; even more gathered in Harlan County in 1931 to protest the miners' situation. Having learned to show their support during the 1920s protests over the Sacco and Vanzetti convictions and impending executions, writers and other citizens sympathetic to liberal causes saw themselves as a strong moral force for change in sometimes corrupt American class-based politics. The feeling was hardly new: Edward Dahlberg, Waldo Frank, William Carlos Williams, and many others had been writing about these problems (and what they saw as solutions) for most of the 1920s. What was new was the physical manifestation of concern and of opinion—the sheer presence of the writer on site.

Marching to protest the Sacco and Vanzetti trial and verdict could be done in Boston (northern, urban America). Marching to protest the convictions of the nine black boys and men in Scottsboro in 1931 could be done in Harlem, with white liberals and writers joining the crowd of intent blacks—and serve as racial protest as well. Marching, marching (as the title of Weatherwax's 1935 novel reminded the reader) was simultaneously a sign of unity, a way of committing to brotherhood and sisterhood, and a sign of displeasure with the establishment. While many American writers were from a middle- or upper-class background and seldom in danger themselves of the poverty they experienced vicariously through their efforts in these protests against industrial practices, they used the condition of the lower-class worker as a metaphor to express their own discontent with their country.

Back home again after years of expatriation, American writers were caught between a nostalgic memory of what their earlier years in the country had seemed to be and what they saw in the towns and roads around them. Not everyone who had a Harvard degree (as did John Dos Passos, James Agee, e. e. cummings, John Peale Bishop, Scofield Thayer) had been to the south end of Boston: for them, seeing the deadly and largely unquestioned poverty of mill workers and sharecroppers in North Carolina or Tennessee was a new kind of education. The attraction of the documentary photograph (and film) was that it could bring these indescribable living conditions into the ken of interested observers.

Returning to America also meant, implicitly, accepting the premises of the American dream. Young writers returned from Europe in part to settle down—to have a family, a home, a conventional church-based existence in some small town—or to lead a more costly life in some urban, and therefore more cosmopolitan, setting complete with dance concerts, symphonies, plays, and fine restaurants where French was still mandated for ordering meals. Not only did these writers discover that securing such lives for themselves would be difficult; they found to their surprise that very few Americans could attain those lifestyles. Friends from their adolescence were dead, killed from accidents as they rode the rails. Other acquaintances were dead from overdoses, or from alcoholism, as well as from military service. Marriages, when they occurred, were battlegrounds for financial wars over how much the mortgage payment could be, where children's clothes would be purchased, or how many nights a month parents could frolic. A culture in transition creates as many casualties as outright war.

The discrepancy between the America the expatriates returned to and the one they envisioned as the country they had left—sometimes more than a decade before—jarred them into looking more critically at their surroundings. Subscriptions to the magazines and journals that dared to criticize the country (*The New Republic, Anvil, Partisan Review, The Nation,* and particularly *The New Masses*) increased, and even writers who thought themselves apolitical submitted manuscripts to those publications. Everybody had something to say about America as it had become, the new America; everybody saw that America falling short of the idealized promise that seemed to peak at the close of World War I.

No one wanted to admit that this nostalgic view had been wrong from the start—that the conditions that so shocked the observers in Harlan County or Akron, Ohio, had existed during the 1920s as well as the 1930s. Industrialization had always meant abuses of labor (and would continue to mean that, until the National Labor Relations Board [NLRB] achieved the law mandating a 40-hour-work week in 1940. Once the law was in place, however, enforcing it took another decade—at least). There would be little reason to stop writing the labor novel, the strike novel, the collective novel. And those forms have continued, though seldom identified as such, into the present. So have the abuses of labor and industrialization.

As we have seen, because so much attention was focused on the poor of America, the character of the American novel changed radically. Earlier critical paradigms became inadequate for judging contemporary fiction. The bewilderment some readers felt as they paused in horror at Albert Maltz's description of the torture of a young auto worker, taking place in the posh suburbs of Detroit at the hands of wealthy plant managers, was difficult to define in critical terms. As Richard Wright explains in his introduction to Nelson Algren's 1942 novel, *Never Come Morning,*

> Most of us 20th century Americans are reluctant to admit the tragically low quality of experiences of the broad American masses; feverish radio programs, super advertisements, stream-lined skyscrapers, million-dollar movies, and mass production have somehow created the illusion in us that we are "rich" in our emotional lives. To the greater understanding of our times, *Never Come Morning* portrays what actually exists in the nerve, brain, and blood of our boys on the street, be they black, white, native, or foreign-born. I say this for the public record, for there will come a time when the middle class will gasp and say . . . "Why weren't we told this before? Why didn't our novelists depict the beginnings of this terrible thing that has come upon us?"[45]

In Wright's defense of the "terrible" realism American fiction was creating, he establishes the battle between earlier standards of literary conventions in the novel and the forms, and languages, felt to be appropriate for conveying the times as they occurred during the Depression. Whatever traditions a reader valued in American fiction, the work of the 1930s and the early 1940s had probably moved away from them. In Algren's novel, for example, Bruno Bicek, the young Polish would-be fighter, lives a life of petty crime and sexual intimidation. What starts out as Bicek's romance with the young Steffi Rostenkowski ends with his giving her to his gang members. Her rape by the half-dozen men, with another dozen lined up waiting as Bicek drinks himself into oblivion, stretches through several sections of the book. "Rescued" by the powerful and thoroughly corrupt old barber who runs the street, Steffi becomes a prostitute. The novel ends with the arrest of Bicek, finally charged with the earlier murder of a young Greek man, walking handcuffed past his gang and saying somberly, "Knew I'd never get t' be twenty-one anyhow."[46] Readers found themselves having to adjust to harsh acts, harsh speech, and rough characters. The act of reading American fiction was undergoing immense changes.

3

Wars of All Kinds

Rather than seeing the 1940s as an extension of the 1930s, most critics equate the latter decade with the conflict—and the eventual national prosperity—of World War II. For Americans, however, the Second World War did not even begin until the Japanese attacked Pearl Harbor in December 1941. It was another year before industry was fully mobilized—working more often on the labor of untrained women and girls than on that of the men who customarily ran industrial machines. And it was another three years before the war ended. One of the results of wartime industrial effort was a severe paper shortage: publishing anything was difficult during the early 1940s.

The writing that was published early in the 1940s, then, was likely to be by established writers—and, therefore, might well continue the direction of 1930s fiction. Just as Ernest Hemingway's *For Whom the Bell Tolls** (1940) blends proletarian themes from his *To Have and Have Not* with the antiwar narrative of *A Farewell to Arms,* so Albert Halper's *Sons of the Fathers* (1940) reflects the style and stories of early twentieth-century immigrant life in Chicago, stories which he had told in both *The Foundry* and *The Chute.* Begun in 1937, *Sons of the Fathers* describes the life of the Saul Bergman family as the Depression forces the immigrant father to lose his small grocery store. Economic conditions improve as war begins but Saul—afraid his sons will have to fight in a war that is largely Europe's—is horrified at Hitler's invasion of Belgium. Following the older sons, Milt and Ben, the narrative shows how society judges men who make unpatriotic decisions. Ben, the better educated of the two, takes a draft-exempt job; Milt enlists in the Army. After Milt's good friend is killed, however, he speaks at the synagogue about his own reluctance to fight: "as I see it, this country has been dragged into a war which doesn't concern its people at all . . . and a lot of fine words

---

*A brief chapter on literature from 1940 to 1945, including this work, appears in my *Modern American Novel, 1914–1945.*

have been put forth to cover things up." He continues despite the stir of protest and a call of "Traitor": "I for one do not now believe in the war. But I'm a soldier who has taken his oath and I'm not backing out. But I feel that the war is all wrong, that the young men of this country are being butchered in vain . . . "[1]

As Milt, his girlfriend, and Ben are run out of the building, Halper suggests that it is Saul's ambivalence about the war that has shaped Milt's attitude. Later, when Milt is killed in action in France just days before Germany's surrender, Saul mourns his firstborn with the self-scrutiny that gives the book its title. He also curses the blind nationalism that this war has instilled in the young, predicting that in another generation "the stink of fine words and patriotism will again perfume the atmosphere!"[2]

Though a prescient novel about a war which had not yet begun, *Sons of the Fathers* shares with other works by writers who had come of age during the Depression the vision of an American culture that could not be honest with itself because what it saw was too fearful. This is the tone of Pietro Di Donato's *Christ in Concrete* (1939), the excruciating narrative set in New York of Italian-American construction workers killed as the building they are working in crumbles upon them; of William Attaway's *Let Me Breathe Thunder* (1939)—in which he describes the hobo life of two young tramps trying to care for a young Mexican boy while they ride the rails— and his *Blood on the Forge* (1941), which is about southern blacks vying for jobs in the northern steel mills; and even of F. Scott Fitzgerald's *The Last Tycoon* (1941). In all of these late 1930s and early 1940s works, any promise that might have been found in America is presented as dead, defeated by circumstances both economic and moral.

Historian Richard H. Pells sees the complexities surrounding the change from the liberal sentiments of the 1930s—when all readers at least understood what progressives/communists were aiming for, whether or not they agreed with those aims—as part of the layered philosophical fabric of a country moving from a failed idealism to a new, less open kind of pragmatism. Assuming that there was an American dream to be attained meant that all occupations were promising: any work, any job, was the means by which one succeeded. The 1930s had proved this belief false—or at least oversimplified. But in the place of the "work = success" maxim, Americans called for other myths: "In the late 1930s intellectuals as well as ordinary people were attracted to either-or propositions, yes-or-no answers."[3] According to Pells, many found ambiguity, paradox, and contradiction frightening.

Capitalism American-style was what the country had, and people who had survived the 1930s decided that—rather than face massive change—it could be made to work. Ironically, readers of 1930s liberal fiction quickly turned against the concepts that might have produced "a different social structure and value system—the search for community and the theory of collectivism, the view of society as an organic unit."[4] Rather, according to Pells, the threat of the cataclysmic Second World War "came as a relief from the formidable social and economic problems which neither the intelligentsia nor the government could solve."[5] There was security in joining together against a foreign evil: fascism, not unemployment, became society's whipping boy.

It is this temper of acquiescence to the times, this jump with both feet into the spirit of authoritarian militarism, that Robert Penn Warren critiques in his 1946 *All the King's Men*. Using three narratives— one of the young, well-educated narrator, Jack Burden; another of the politician Willie Starks; and the third an embedded story of Cass Mastern's betrayal of his friend, the husband of his lover, Annabelle Trice—Warren explores the tenuous loyalties among men who are hungry for both acclaim and power. In a network of relationships that stretches through southern history, Warren does much more than rehearse Huey Long's career as Louisiana demagogue—he investigates the way society allows itself to be used by Long/Starks. Under the guise of benefiting his state, Starks abuses the power people vested in him. But so too does the seemingly more innocent Judge Irwin, the man who is Jack's true father. And—Warren points out—so does Jack himself, particularly in his relationships with his childhood friends the Stantons.

Warren has said consistently that the book is not about politics.[6] Based on his earlier play, *Proud Flesh*, which he had written in Italy during 1938 and 1939 "with the news of the war filling the papers and the boot heels of Mussolini's legionnaires clanging on the stones,"[7] *All the King's Men* drew from the atmosphere of trust betrayed—the author suggests that the idealism of a people's belief in fascism is no different from the idealism of Americans trusting democracy. Warren's Pulitzer Prize–winning novel is a study of the way a man's self-identification can blur rational thought. As long as

Jack Burden saw himself as Willie Starks rather than as Judge Irwin, he could not untangle his own allegiances: he could believe Willie's rhetoric about providing medical care even as he watched the man's clearly abusive manipulations of power. As long as he self-righteously disdained his mother's life, he could deny his own need for love.

The novel draws obviously on fiction of the 1930s in its portrayal of man lost, rootless. Community in Warren's fiction becomes a site for the uses of others, not a place for nurturing. Jack Burden's alien-ation from his past, then, seems less neurotic to those of Warren's readers who had experienced both the 1930s and 1930s fiction.

Warren also takes the voice of the wanderer as his narrator. Told in the distinctive idiom of the young Burden, the male-storied account of life on the run reads like a tale of poverty or displace-ment or hunger. The book opens,

MASON CITY.
To get there you follow Highway 58, going northeast out of the city, and it is a good highway and new. Or was new, that day we went up it. You look up the highway and it is straight for miles, coming at you, with the black line down the center coming at and at you, black and slick and tarry-shining against the white of the slab, and the heat dazzles up from the white slab so that only the black line is clear, coming at you with the whine of the tires, and if you don't quit staring at that line and don't take a few deep breaths and slap yourself hard on the back of the neck you'll hypnotize yourself and you'll come to just at the moment when the right front wheel hooks over into the black dirt shoulder off the slab.[8]

Incorrigibly colloquial, Burden's voice tells the pseudocomic story of Willie's making great use of the photo-op in his hometown (Mason City) drugstore. It then carries the long story down to its postscript—Willie is dead, and Jack is married, living in his true father's house, providing a home for the old man he had believed was his father, and meditating on the traditionally anxious father-son bond. In fact, the novel suggests that knowledge of the truth of one's parentage may be nearly meaningless information: as Jack says in his closing monologue, "each of us is the son of a million fathers."[9]

For all the identification of men with parents and of parents with offspring, the lines of descent from the patriarchy in Warren's novel are as muddied and muddled as anywhere else in modern letters.

Unearthing the truth means as little to Jack Burden—despite his Ph.D. in history and his admonitory reading of Cass Mastern's life—as it does to Willie Starks. What history finally teaches is that men die, and when they die, their sons scarcely mourn them.

The World War II Novel

All the King's Men adumbrates the pervasive themes of many American World War II novels through its steady emphasis on male authority, male-male relationships, and the uses and abuses of power. War novels are naturally fictions about men's lives; often, what women characters they contain are the lovers and mothers the men remember and, in memory, often dignify and idealize. But the struggle for selfhood and/or identity, and any power that might result from that conflict, has to occur among men. As critic Chester E. Eisinger points out, "The rebellion against mindless, arbitrary authority, which had been directed against the police in the thirties, was directed, in the war novels, against the officer class."[10]

Both Joseph J. Waldmeir and Eisinger conclude that novelists of the Second World War were influenced as much by 1930s fiction as they were by the novels of the First World War. Eisinger writes,

The war novelist was sensitive to injustice and compassionate toward those who were wronged or victimized by the military machine. The engagement of his mind and his emotions with the problems of what have been called the ritualistic victims of our culture—Negroes and Jews—is a mark of his indebtedness to the thirties.[11]

Many of these works about war, Eisinger continues, are despairing because the authors recognized—as writers also did during the 1930s—that "democratic and humane conceptions"[12] no longer existed. Whether the blanket of sheer poverty had dampened hope or whether a frequently mindless militarism had inhibited it, writers who described the modern culture found little of promise.

The title of Norman Mailer's *The Naked and the Dead* (1948) signals his acceptance of that bleak view. Creating an epic format so that he could write about a panorama of men, all caught in a military action he labels futile from the start, Mailer forces the reader to question the premises of not only war, but of war fiction. Recounting the stories of what the author terms the "bunch of dispossessed" men who comprised the 1940s military was in no way an optimistic task. Both in his detailed descriptions of the war theater on the Pacific island and in the contrastingly subjective "Time Machine" autobiographies, Mailer includes a wide array of American men—Brooklyn Jews, Polish Chicagoans, Boston Irish, Texans, Mexicans, poor southerners. Regardless of their place of origin, their education, their incomes, their ethnicity and religious beliefs, and their politics, if characters were enlisted men, they were all headed for the same outcome.

When Lt. Robert Hearn dies on a reconnaissance mission his men know is both doomed and useless, his personal struggle against the larger forces of the military (personified in Major General George Cummings, whom Hearn refers to as "Generalissimo") becomes clear. Mailer shows that Cummings and his ideological offspring like Jesse Croft—whose cruel delayed killing of a Japanese survivor reveals his immorality—would eventually dominate the battlefield. As Waldmeir writes, Croft "represents the physical aspect of Fascism as Cummings represents the intellectual, and on his own level, he desires power as strongly as does Cummings. He alone has commanded the platoon since the invasion and the death of its commanding officer, and he so resents the fact that Hearn has been placed over him that he purposely holds back scouting information about a Japanese machine-gun emplacement and lets Hearn walk directly into point-blank range."[13]

Beginning with the confused flight of the young soldier Hennessey on the beach at Anapopei, *The Naked and the Dead* shows the inevitability of death for these powerless enlisted men. Taking orders is all they can do. Mailer's novel fits in part into the thematic pattern of war novels that criticize the officer class, but it also creates a number of enlisted men who are inferior beings—such as the racist bully Roy Gallagher.

In 1948, some critics and readers were so incensed by what they saw as Mailer's sensationalized, derogatory portraits of Americans in the military that Robert C. Healey's criticism was fairly common. Healey notes that, according to these accounts of World War II, "the ordinary American fighting man was sex-mad, unscrupulous and completely insensitive, the end-product of a vicious society, and his officers were either fascists or incompetents or both, though the fascists are usually depicted as very competent and intelligent in gain-ing their ends."[14] While the language of the war novel is cleaner than that of the fiction to come in the 1960s and the 1970s (Mailer regularly uses *fug* and *fuggin'*, for example), there is an unrelievedly sexist prescription for depicting women characters, and racism and anti-Semitism are givens. In Mailer's novel, Jewish characters such as Roth and Goldstein exist in part to show that deep-seated prejudice.

Irwin Shaw's *The Young Lions*, also published in 1948, also rehearses ideological differences between fascism and democracy. This novel is often considered to be positive—perhaps by dividing the narrative among three protagonists, Shaw keeps reader interest through greater variety. While Noah Ackerman and Michael Whitacre are Americans, Christian Diestl is an Austrian Nazi. All are young, intelligent, and in some ways thoughtful.

The author works hard in the book's opening to show that Diestl, a ski instructor, is a vast improvement over the innkeeper's son, Frederick, who attempts to rape Margaret Freemantle after a New Year's celebration. Yet both men are Nazis. An American skier awaiting her Jewish lover at the Austrian resort in 1938, Margaret realizes that Europe is already unsafe for both her and her lover. When she flees the inn and waits at the train station to meet Joseph, Diestl talks with her about fascism. Explaining its hold on the poor of Germany and Austria, he comforts her by saying that the persecution of Jews is only a means to the end of improving Europe, "an unlucky accident. Somehow, someone discovered that that was the only way to come to power. I am not saying I like it. Myself, I know it is ridiculous to attack any race. Myself, I know there are Jews like Frederick, and Jews, say, like myself. But if the only way you can get a decent and ordered Europe is by wiping out the Jews, then we must do it. A little injustice for a large justice. . . . the end justifies the means."[15] At Margaret's expression of horror, he reassures her, "I promise you something. It will never come to that. You can tell your friend that, too. For a year or two, he will be a little annoyed. He may have to give up his business; he may have to move from his house. But once the thing is accomplished, once the trick has done what it is intended to do, he will be restored. The Jew is a means, not an end."[16]

Lest readers in 1948 had forgotten the Holocaust (or, in some parts of American culture, disbelieved its existence), contemporary novels about World War II both directly and subtly raise the issue of anti-Semitism. Nearly every war novel includes a Jew among its characters, and that figure is often the liberal, humane man of the group. In contrast to what appears to be a steady emphasis on Jewish characters and the anti-Semitism their presence usually evokes, black military figures are almost nonexistent. The writings of William Rollins Jr. (particularly his 1938 Spanish Civil War novel, *The Wall of Men*) and John O. Killens (his 1962 *And Then We Heard the Thunder,* a moving story of a black company, takes the reader from basic training through combat to a race riot in Australia) are exceptions. In these books, the reader empathizes with the black characters who are virtually isolated from and at times prohibited from fighting in the war.

Although the critical view of Shaw's *The Young Lions* is that it provides a more positive than usual view of men at war, the book ends with the German retreat. In one of his last acts, the German sniper Diestl kills the unwary Ackerman; his friend Whitacre then kills the Austrian. As in *The Naked and the Dead,* here too the war ends more by luck than because of superior Allied military talent. Whitacre's shot at point-blank range at the wounded Diestl is hardly ameliorative, but it could be that the Austrian's death, execution style, can be read as symbolizing the death of Fascism.

That readers so close in time to the war itself wanted the fiction of World War II to be ideologically based makes sense. Fascism was defeated; democracy still existed. The Allied forces *had* won, and despite the international controversy over the use of atomic bombs in destroying Hiroshima and Nagasaki, most American readers felt satisfied if not exuberantly victorious. The political agenda for novels published during the 1940s and early 1950s, then, was to praise the democratic system even while admitting that the military organization per se, because of its need to command, bordered on fascism itself. James Gould Cozzens's *Guard of Honor,* another 1948 novel, comes down on the side of nihilism when the author unveils the damning falsity of its prototypical liberal, Jim Edsell.

As we have seen, one way writers shaped narrative to question the power of military organization was to set officers against enlisted men. Differences in class, or at least in education, were clearly visible. For the most part officers spoke better, knew more, and had led more sophisticated lives. They were from a higher class, and their military service was motivated by patriotism. Enlisted men and noncoms, in contrast, were often seeking work, place, and stability by joining the armed services—or so their fictional portraits suggest. As critic Robert Healey comments, it is frequently the case in war novels that young male characters "are presented as the lonely, restless children of the Depression."[17]

The depiction of enlisted men as innocent youths, while in some ways a sentimental ploy, quickly made villains out of the officer class. True to that oversimplified dichotomy, many officers in war novels are drawn as being little more than appetites, appetites for power. William Styron's *The Long March* (1952) is a paradigmatic narrative for the conflict between the officers who can give whatever orders they choose and the marines who must obey those orders. Set in a Carolina training camp during the summer of 1950, with its military personnel drawn from reservists (veterans of the Second World War who have been recalled for the Korean "police action"), the novella recounts events on the swelteringly brutal 36-mile march that Colonel Templeton has ordered.

With the stable Lieutenant Culver as narrator, Styron draws the cool colonel (who marches with his men till almost the end of the trek) as the focus for the hatred of Captain Al Mannix, a Brooklyn reservist whose return to the military has meant the loss of his business. Angry that his wife and children are deprived of both his presence and his income, Mannix sports the inflammatory temper of the marginalized—his Jewishness is a key element in his personality. As Styron presents Mannix, his competitive urgency becomes his primary quality. His friend Culver worries that his completing the long march may lead to illness, if not death.

A small episode in war history, Templeton's march is itself overshadowed by the deaths of eight soldiers just before the exercise, deaths that are caused by two mortar shells exploding in the midst of a mess line. The novella begins with the deaths of those eight innocent "boys . . . shreds of bone, gut, and dangling tissue"[18] and the impact of those deaths on Templeton's company. In this context, it is possible that the somewhat absurd march is a diversionary tactic, a way to keep the company (comprised largely of veterans resentful about being called back) from thinking too steadily about the hazards of their current military service.

Styron does not excuse Templeton, however. As he watches Mannix while he tries not to overreact to the assignment, the author shows the colonel's surprise at the fierce antagonism the march has evoked in the Brooklyn captain. Mannix determines that he will "make the last six miles out of pride and spite. Out of fury. It was a seedy, bedraggled column of people: of hollow, staring eyes and faces green with slack-jawed exhaustion."[19] Without thinking back to Mannix's insubordinate remarks during training sessions, Templeton knows that this man is a possible problem, "no longer a simple doubter but the heretic."[20] The plot of the novella, then, is psychological: will Mannix break, and if he does, will he affront his commanding officer Templeton so that he will have to be court-martialed?

Like Thomas Heggen's *Mr. Roberts, The Long March* poses questions that have complex answers. So too does Herman Wouk's 1951 *The Caine Mutiny*, and the fascination of that novel (and films) depends again on the psychological force of the battle of wills between Lt. Commander Philip F. Queeg, captain of the minesweeper *Caine*, and would-be novelist Lieutenant Keefer, one of the several leaders of the mutiny. Another central character is Lt. Maryk, executive officer, because he faces the dilemma of proving Queeg incapacitated, unstable, perhaps paranoid (by keeping a journal of his commander's acts) while simultaneously allowing him to keep command of the ship. During the climactic hours of a typhoon, however, when Queeg's orders become contradictory, Maryk takes over—but is then charged with mutinous action. Keefer, by this time, has withdrawn his earlier protests against Queeg's command.

Wouk intends at the end of the work to try to salvage the military system from criticism. The strange statements of defense attorney Lt. Greenwald, who gets the charge of mutiny dismissed and frees Maryk, undermine Queeg's characterization throughout the book. After the trial Greenwald theorizes that military personnel must be absolutely authoritarian, absolutely code-bound, regardless of what appears to be sane or insane behavior, saying to Keefer, whose novel is about to be published: "Queeg deserved better at my hands."[21] Because the backbone of the military are the "regulars—these stuffy, stupid Prussians, in the Navy and the Army," Greenwald continues, "if I wrote a war novel I'd try to make a hero out of Old Yellowstain [Queeg]."[22] He believes that both Maryk and himself will be held in suspicion after this trial but that Keefer (who testified, in effect, against Maryk) will maintain his good reputation, even though his novel criticizes the Navy.

That same year, 1951, James Jones's *From Here to Eternity* tackled a similar kind of power dilemma in telling the story of a lone soldier. The book is the odyssey of young Robert E. Lee Prewitt, a naive southerner whose concept of battle is simultaneously too idealistic and too humane. Drawing the soldier as the protagonist of a bildungsroman, in the tradition of Stephen Crane's *The Red Badge of Courage* (1895), is an approach that allows the author some autobiographical empathy. As critic Peter G. Jones writes, "going to war is almost always the first great 'adventure' of life, the primary movement from home into the world beyond."[23] What makes *From Here to Eternity* such a fine book, this critic argues, is that Jones "successfully universalizes Prewitt's experience."[24]

One might disagree with the critic's emphasis on this abstracted meaning. After all, Prewitt is a renegade, a man the opposite of what readers would consider the good soldier. In fact, what makes *From Here to Eternity* so memorable is the graphically impossible situations Prewitt gets himself into—and allows himself to be killed because of. Since Prewitt has learned the lessons of military training well, he can predict when what he does is extreme enough to earn punishment. Rather than being the docile southerner who doesn't understand the implications of his actions, Prewitt plays the system against itself. He manipulates the military, knowing that the military mind acts—and must act—in certain ways.

Prewitt's story begins on the site of the eternal Depression, in the poverty of Harlan County, Kentucky, and its remorseless Christianity. Promising his dying mother that he will never willingly hurt anyone, Prewitt finds himself, after he joins the army, made into a boxer. After he blinds a man during a match, he gives up boxing; the military, however, won't let him retire. The aimless soldier finds himself running from his guilt over his broken promise to his mother, only to land in Captain Dynamite Holmes "G" Company—where he will again be forced to box.

Countless episodes of Prewitt's insubordination (that is, pride) make him a regular in Major Thompson's brutal stockade. While there, he witnesses the incredible beating death of his friend Blues Berry by Fatso Judson. After Prewitt is released, he feels honor bound to avenge Berry's death and takes on—and kills—Fatso in a fair fight. From that point on, Jones makes clear that Prewitt's own interpretation of his life will lead to his death.

The bombing of Pearl Harbor brings Prewitt back to his company from his outlaw, AWOL status. But because he does not have proper identification when he tries to return, the military police—dismayed at his running from their commands—shoot and kill him.

John Hersey's powerful *The War Lover* also takes as its central consciousness, and hero, a young southern officer, Charles Boman. Just as the figure of the intellectual outsider, often Jewish, had become a stock character for war novels, so had the naive, good, slow and often dumb southerner. Hersey's southerner is not slow, however; he lacks only the kind of self-confidence that leads men like his pilot-buddy, Buzz Marrow, to be a hero. Boman's modesty is what the British woman Daphne loves in him, and her choosing the copilot over Marrow, the man who loves war, accounts for much of the novel's action.

Boman as the narrative voice remains in the background of the novel's action, while portraits of Marrow during his various "brave" exploits constitute much of the story. Hersey is careful to introduce the two characters differently, however, mentioning frequently the displeasure Boman causes Marrow—for example, "Buzz was staring across at me. His face was white and broad and too big, and it wore an appalling look of disapproval."[25] Even though this is Boman's recollection of a dream conflict, Hersey uses it to reinforce his initial characterization of Marrow as robot, one whose inhumanity will lead to his downfall:

Marrow was being Marrow; a hunk of machinery, concerned only with his work, which was to drive twenty-seven tons of metal up a road of thin air. . . . his face was no more and no less expressive than the altimeter or one of the r.p.m. indicators. His eyes moved without haste from dial to dial, and at times he looked out at the shoals of atmosphere beneath us, or at the gaps of toplessness in the clouds above—but in a calculating and not a sensuous way. . . . He was calm and automatic.[26]

By 1959, when Hersey took on the difficult task of implying that some men—often, heroic ones—liked the brutality of war too much, a number of new considerations fed into readers' assessments of war fiction. Even though critics had agreed that fiction about World War II and the Korean conflict was varied, it seldom deviated from the plots of enlisted men vs. officers or bildungsromane that described the initiatory experiences of young American fighting men. For Hersey to avoid the now-stereotypical alignments within the genre, writing about men no longer naive, both of them officers, was taking on the challenge of remaking the war novel.

Hersey approached this task with both seriousness and the experience of his previous writing about war. In 1942, he had published his war correspondent's account, *Men on Bataan,* and the next year, his *Into the Valley* reported on a Gaudalcanal skirmish. In 1944, his novel *A Bell for Adano* charted ideological differences between living in Italy under fascism and then democracy (and won the Pulitzer Prize for fiction); his 1946 *Hiroshima* used the techniques of objective reporting to assess the horrors of the bombing. In 1950, his intricate novel *The Wall* insisted on a range of motivation for human behavior, this time in the Warsaw ghetto as the Germans decimated the Jews. Hersey knew how to report, how to use ethnography, how to write fiction—and he did all these things in his carefully structured 1959 novel.

The War Lover alternates between compelling accounts of "the raid," from 0200 through 1739 hours, and the company's tour of duty, March 1 through August 1, leading up to the day of the raid. "The raid," made over Germany during daylight hours, is memorable for its heavy Allied losses and casualties—and for Marrow's breakdown—"the tour" is the interwoven story of the ten men bound to the plane, which had been named *The Body* (one result of Marrow's insolent equation of sexuality with bravery). As Boman recounts episodes from the men's lives while they are stationed in England, the reader can sort through the continuum of war-haters to war-lovers. One particularly interesting narrative is of Boman's romance with Daphne, a liaison always threatened by Marrow's competitive sexuality. The reader understands that Buzz does not love Daphne; he just wants whatever his copilot already has.

The closing of the longer narrative focuses on Marrow's attempt to rape Daphne, and her account of his impotence directly foreshadows his breakdown at the controls of *The Body.* That Marrow chooses death in the sea rather than survival with the other men seems a fitting denouement for a character who lived his life entirely for the satisfaction of killing. In 1959, *The War Lover* could be admonitory in ways that war novels written during the 1940s and early 1950s could not have been: to criticize the passions that turned men into heroes might well have been seen as unpatriotic.

For the most part, World War II novels were written by people who had experienced the conflict either as combatants or correspondents. Shaw, Mailer, Jones, Styron, and Hersey were all young writers, men from the generation following the modernists and the writers of the 1930s. Even as William Faulkner worked throughout the 1940s on the book that was to be his reaction to World War II,

A Fable (1954), many other established novelists did not successfully attempt work that could be described as war fiction. Hemingway had made a good start with *For Whom the Bell Tolls,* but his
later *Across the River and into the Trees* (1950) is remote from his best
writing.

For John Steinbeck, too, whose reputation rested on *In Dubious
Battle* and, more prominently, *The Grapes of Wrath,* turning to war-
related fiction seemed difficult. His 1942 *The Moon Is Down,* while it
focuses on Nazi sensibility, is weaker than *Cannery Row* (1945) and
The Wayward Bus (1947). Albert Maltz, whose *Underground Stream*
appeared in 1940, wrote a psychological study of German characters
in *The Cross and the Arrow* (1944). Although he had changed nation-
alities of his characters, Maltz was once again intrigued with the
assessment of power among men—who had it, what lengths they
would go to use it and keep it, and what nationality had to do with
moral and ethical practices.

Novels at the Periphery of War

As they would in 1949 with John Hawkes's *The Cannibal,* critics in
1944 found Saul Bellow's *Dangling Man* an example of American-
style existentialism. After Albert Camus's *L'Étranger* appeared in
1942, it became a point of comparison for subsequent terse, experimental writing throughout the world. Bleakly elliptical, the two
American books spin nonchronological narratives out of the desperation of wartime ennui: here, emotional tone is more significant
than plot. *The Cannibal* takes the form of a Kafkaesque parable, with
widely separated scenes set in Germany during both World War I
and World War II.

Dangling Man, another first novel, uses the plausible situation of a
man's resigning his job because he is being drafted. Because Joseph
is Canadian, however, his security clearance takes months, and
meanwhile—living on his wife's income, alone in their apartment—
he is overcome by "a narcotic dullness. . . . I think of myself as a
moral casualty of the war."[27] Written as Joseph's diary, Bellow's
account of a man cut loose from work and, therefore, identity is
understated and poignant. And when a third-person voice (that of
an imaginary older Joseph) takes over as narrator, except for the
change in the narrative from "I" to "he," there is no difference in

voice or intensity. The latter narrator writes, "Joseph suffers from a feeling of strangeness, of not quite belonging to the world, of lying under a cloud and looking up at it."[28] Back in first person a few entries later, Joseph writes, "Slept until eleven o'clock; sat around all afternoon and thought of nothing in particular."[29] A few weeks later, after Christmas, his entry reads, "Slept until one o'clock. Out at four for a walk, I lasted ten minutes and then retreated."[30] The first-person entries illustrate the larger observations of the "other" Joseph as narrator.

The drama in Bellow's novel occurs in the real civilian world that Joseph is trying to avoid. His obvious differences with his ambitious brother, Amos, and his own family, particularly his daughter, Etta, form one strand of the plot. Ironically, between the two entries quoted above, where Joseph's withdrawal from life is the apparent theme, Etta accuses her uncle of sexually molesting her. The reactions of the family and of Iva, Joseph's wife, appear only obliquely—Joseph himself seems untouched by Etta's accusations.

Later, however, Bellow's narrative makes clear that Joseph relishes the charges. Just as he reads the lists of men dead in action, defining himself exclusively as a military man, so he ponders what "life" is. For him as he waits out this stasis, "days have lost their distinctiveness."[31] As he considers what he calls this "derangement of days, the leveling of occasions,"[32] he concludes, "Trouble, like physical pain, makes us actively aware that we are living."[33] For the reader already familiar with Camus's Meursault or Kafka's Josef K., Bellow's Joseph seems to be an existential clone. About the war he announces, "Myself, I would rather die in the war than consume its benefits. . . . I would rather be a victim[34] than a beneficiary."[35]

It is with a relief echoing Joseph's own that the reader follows him into the military. Although Joseph's diary entry on his last day as a civilian stresses his comfort ("I am no longer to be held accountable for myself"[36]), Bellow has made clear that the "lives" of people surrounding Joseph—including those of his wife and family—lack either interest or humanity. When he celebrates his new condition of "regimentation," then, Joseph in effect denounces both the American dream and the myth of individual freedom under democracy.

The presence of World War II and Korea—what Joseph calls "what the rest of my generation is undergoing"[37]—becomes the seldom described background for other midcentury novels, those as apparently different from each other as Paul Bowles's *The Sheltering*

Sky (1949), John Updike's *Rabbit, Run* (1960), and Walker Percy's *The Moviegoer* (1960). In each novel, the protagonist is either running from the consequences of a self-knowledge buried under the debris of military service (usually, that of personal fear and a cringing from combat) or avoiding the very thought of that period of his life. Port Moresby turns to exotic travel (along with drink, drugs, and dangerous sexual liaisons); Rabbit Angstrom literally runs away from the predictable, respectable life he chose for himself, and Binx Bolling cannot even begin the human life he and his family had expected him to lead. It is as if Ernest Hemingway's postwar angst, described so thoughtfully if cryptically in his 1926 *The Sun Also Rises*, had been a primary influence on these younger male writers in content as well as in style.

Bowles's *The Sheltering Sky* illustrates nihilism writ large. Port and Kit Moresby are each unconnected from life—including most clearly their marriage. Surrounded by a drifting postwar malaise, the Moresbys war with each other, Port searching for sex with anyone but Kit, and Kit feigning an interest in other men, such as Tunner. The mood of meaningless ennui is familiar; the novel opens,

He awoke, opened his eyes. The room meant very little to him; he was too deeply immersed in the non-being from which he had just come. If he had not the energy to ascertain his position in time and space, he also lacked the desire. He was somewhere, he had come back through vast regions from nowhere; there was the certitude of an infinite sadness at the core of his consciousness, but the sadness was reassuring, because it alone was familiar. . . .[38]

Another victim of that ultimate betrayal, the war that caused such undefinable self-loathing, Port spends his time moving from place to place ("he would begin to plan some new, impossible trip"). He had traveled before the war, but now he studies maps with a different purpose: he did not want any reminders of war; in fact, he admitted that "war was one facet of the mechanized age he wanted to forget."[39]

In North Africa, however, where the book opens, war had left its mark. Kit notes as they drink in the open cafe, "the whole horrible thing that happens after every war, everywhere." The uniformity of despairing cultures depresses her as much as it does Port; as the Spanish maid at the hotel remarks, "La vida es pena."[40] Port and Kit intellectually understand such suffering, but they seem incapable of helping each other. Although they have been married for a dozen years, Bowles's novel tells their distinctly separate stories.

Port's late-night hegira into a lonely Arab camp leaves him the likely prey of thieves and killers. Later, his slow death of a mysterious fever, in the midst of a meningitis epidemic, forces Kit to abandon him. Bowles focuses on her distraught yet crafty derangement as she escapes from his cell of death into the Sahara—from which dark night of the soul she returns mad. "You should never think of what is finished,"[41] her black lover Amar tells her as she cries, trying vainly to avoid the flood of pain that memories of Port—and her odyssey in the desert—bring her.

In Bowles's 1949 novel, Kit at least has memories that bring her excruciating pain. By 1960, when John Updike wrote the first of his Rabbit Angstrom novels (*Rabbit, Run*), his war survivor and former basketball star protagonist had learned to defeat even his pain at his child's death. Running from his wife, running from his lover, running from friendship, and finally running from his infant daughter's funeral, Rabbit refuses any attempt to reach his angry pain. "It was the Army," his mother explains to the concerned minister as his family tries to piece together Rabbit's reasons for leaving his wife so precipitously: "When he came back from Texas he was a different boy."[42] References hidden in the busy text of Rabbit's aimless running build the untold story of a set of war experiences that hinge on his first girlfriend's marrying someone else ("She married when he was in the Army; a P.S. in a letter from his mother shoved him out from shore. That day he was launched"[43]), as well as his own disorientation as he is cut off from the only thing he was good at, playing basketball. All his memories of Texas, even the sexual ones, are unpleasant.

For Walker Percy's moviegoer, Binx (Jack) Bolling, his relentlessly ordered life—managing an investment office in the suburbs, having predictable affairs with his secretaries, seeing movies—is the way he copes with the trauma of his devastating war wound. So classic is Binx's avoidance of the real that his entire reference pattern depends on films he has seen (he particularly likes the actors Orson Welles, John Wayne, Gregory Peck, and William Holden). Yet his beautiful cousin, Kate Cutrer, is increasingly suicidal after the tragic death of her fiancé. Agoraphobic, drug dependent, and paranoiac, Kate tries to marry the stable Walter but finds herself only deeper in despair. The index to Percy's condemnation in *The Moviegoer* of his protagonist, who is supposedly Kate's confidante, is that Binx does nothing at all to keep her alive. He is seemingly blind to even her suicide attempts.

Kate, rather, wills herself to live by giving Binx a reason for *his* life: they are to marry. He is, then, to give her explicit directions for her every act; in the larger world, he is to give up his crass money-making and go to medical school. Together, then, they will become a useful couple. At least they will stay alive.

Percy's deft paralleling of Kate with Binx makes them both wounded survivors. As Kate reminds him early in the book, "You're like me, but worse. Much worse."[44] A subsequent scene explores more fully Kate's denial, and there Percy repeats the point. Kate's real knowledge of her self and her depression gives her insight into Binx's malaise, as she says matter-of-factly: the accident "gave me my life. That's my secret, just as the war is your secret. . . . Because afterwards everyone said: what a frightful experience she went through and doesn't she do remarkably well. So then I did very well indeed. I would have made a good soldier." When Binx asks her why she would want to be such a thing, she replies cannily if not sanely, "How simple it would be to fight. What a pleasant thing it must be to be among people who are afraid for the first time when you yourself for the first time in your life have a proper flesh-and-blood enemy to be afraid of. What a lark! Isn't that the secret of heroes?" Binx replies, "I couldn't say. I wasn't a hero."[45] He tries to bring the depressing conversation back to some kind of reality. Although he pretends to hear the words Kate literally says, he knows full well what she is suggesting with her comment about "a proper flesh-and-blood enemy." For Kate, as for himself, the enemy is more likely to be some interior consciousness.

In *The Moviegoer*, Percy presents what the reader is to know about Binx's war experiences in the fragmented and elliptical sketches so pervasive in the telling of disorienting stories. Without necessarily being a psychoanalytic critic, the reader is aware that this literary technique conveys the unbearable, that there is a need for elision if not disguise or outright transformation. (The worlds of Kit Moresby and Rabbit Angstrom are surely—at the very least—disguised.) For Binx, the world that nearly ended his existence occurred in "the Orient," at the time of the Korean conflict, and when he came back into consciousness—after being "knocked out for two days"[46]—he found himself under a chindolea bush, "bleeding in a ditch."[47] By leaving amorphous his wounding, Binx's memory deflects even his thought from the military retreat from the Chongchon River, and with it, the episode of his personal betrayal of Ranger company.[48]

The significance in the blockage of his memories of war is that, had it not been for Harold Graebner, Binx's only friend and now the only person with whom he corresponds, he would have died. Cut off after his trauma from more immediate existence, Binx builds connections only with people who have shared his moment of truth—Graebner and, by living through her own trauma, Kate. His world becomes smaller and smaller.

Binx justifies his inertia, another symptom of his post-traumatic hostility to the rest of the world, by creating what he calls "the search." If he had not dedicated himself to his higher (though always unspecified) goal, he would be worn down, entrapped, by what he disdainfully calls "the everydayness"[49] of life. As part of his pose as quester, Binx identifies himself with the Jews, who also define themselves as "exiles"[50]; he also lapses into the dangerous anomie of thinking that "everyone is dead."[51]

Kate is probably right when she says that Binx is "worse" than she. But because he still plays a socially responsible role, making a kind of half-hearted living as a broker (a profession he finds absolutely meaningless, as his vacuous letters to clients show), his family worries less about him than they do about Kate. They at least notice her cries for help—alcohol abuse and drug overdoses—although they are singularly inept in helping her.

Like Kit Moresby of *The Sheltering Sky*, Kate grows to become so male-defined that she cannot find a route to personal happiness without being some man's partner. In these war novels, the coercion of the heterosexual world has inscribed all women—the strong as well as the weak—in almost primitive biological roles. Pictured at its bleakest in Updike's *Rabbit, Run*, the place of even accomplished women like Janice Angstrom, Ruth Leonard, Mrs. Tothero, and the Reverend Eccles's "little wife"[52] is to be sex partner and feeder (Updike's depiction of women as their breasts is consistently unnerving). Similarly, in *Dangling Man*, Iva exists only to normalize the aberrant Joseph. It is a tendency in much postwar fiction by men that the women characters—as Buzz Marrow understands so well—are of interest chiefly because of what sexual dimension they can provide to the male protagonists' narratives. *The Body* names not only Marrow and his crew's plane; it also indexes the place of women characters in fiction written almost exclusively by men.

Surprisingly, building on this set of reader expectations, Updike manages to salvage *Rabbit, Run* and its hardly commendable Angstrom by drawing the women characters in the novel as seriously flawed: Janice drinks; Ruth has been a prostitute; Eccles's wife flirts and wears shorts. If he had presented these women as whole people, reader sympathy for Rabbit would have evaporated. Instead, by concentrating on the women's sexual responses and the way their breasts look after childbirth, Updike succeeds in turning them into only accessories to the real plots. Clearly, in parallel narratives of Tothero, Rev. Eccles, and Angstrom, Updike insists on drawing the male as an immature free agent. Whether justified by beliefs in religion or sports, the men use—and abuse—women (or weaker, less successful men) as they will.

In contrast to Updike's sad portrayal of postwar culture, Walker Percy writes a very different story. For all of Binx's apparent interest in sex, *The Moviegoer* includes no scenes of intercourse. Characters are instead defined by the very "everydayness" Binx pretends to fear. In the Percy world, for one of the rare times in midcentury American fiction, women characters (Binx's Aunt Emily, his mother Anna, Mrs. Boykin Lamar, Kate, Sharon) are responsible and capable. That is the reason one particular interchange between Kate and Binx early in the novel has such resonance. When Kate is describing the car accident in which her fiancé, Lyell, was killed and her ability to leave the accident scene alone, her insistence that she was "happy" as she left (or, rather, that she was alive and able to leave) is at great variance with Binx's saying earlier that his happiest moment in life was "getting out of the army."[53] (We have seen the ways Percy suggests throughout his book that Binx has left neither the army nor its trauma). The image Percy gives the reader of Kate's happy memory, however, is clearly positive: "I just stood there until the door opened, then I got on [the bus] and we went sailing along from bright sunshine down through deep clefts as cool and dark as a springhouse."[54] If physical freedom is an index of hero status, Kate, one of the few strong women characters in midcentury American fiction, has begun to assume that role.

4

American Fiction at War

When the United States emerged from World War II, it was the most powerful nation the world had ever known. It was also the most visible. Free of the immense damage that marred most European and many Asian countries, the United States could see only a panorama of "progress," consisting largely of technological improvements, ahead. The American dream was back in business.

It was no time to make changes in either economic or social arrangements. The union activity of the 1930s fell even further in repute, just as the occupational gains women thought they had made during the war years were substantially erased. Returning military men needed work: the mainstream advertising campaign now was to convince women who had held both blue-collar and white-collar jobs that what they wanted most in life was the chance to become homemakers, wives, and mothers. Predicated on the shortage of men during World War II, the desirability of marriage as the career of choice for women skyrocketed. Fewer women attended college as more and more girls married immediately following high school graduation. During the 1950s, the average marriage age for women dropped to its lowest ever recorded, a stunning 20.3 years of age. The quantity of young families, all bent on having children, meant an equally stunning growth of new housing areas called subdivisions, in new outgrowths of urban areas known as suburbs.

Most literature, however, did not reflect the bouncing optimism that these demographic changes in housing and marriage rates would suggest. As we have seen, a great many writers—most of them men—continued to work with themes and techniques that became popular in the war novel. Others were caught up in the philosophical fascination with existentialism, influenced by the work of Jean-Paul Sartre, Samuel Beckett, and Eugène Ionesco, as well as Albert Camus, writing narrative despite an underlying belief that the actions of life were bereft of explicable meaning. For all the success that the end of the Second World War ostensibly brought, people in the United States were apprehensive: they may not have faced destruction within their own borders, but the advent of nuclear power—especially the vivid images of mushroom clouds as seen on thousands of television screens throughout the country— made them, rightly, nervous.

They were nervous as well because of the onset of the Cold War, a situation which appeared to contradict the Allied victory of World War II. With the Russian blockade of Berlin in 1948, confidence about the United States' place in the international political arena crumbled. Christopher Lasch writes, "The cold war completed the destruction of what hopes had survived the war."[1]

It is difficult to assess in a brief space why the nativism that had occupied so much United States culture during the 1920s returned in the 1950s. What is important is that such sentiment did recur. As conservative forces grew more powerful, any activity that could be judged as critical of democracy was threatening. It was the age of the loyalty oath and of the execution of Ethel and Julius Rosenberg, sent to their deaths as atomic spies. When Joseph McCarthy and his House Un-American Activities Committee began their investigations into the membership of the American Communist Party, a political action that was to ruin the careers and lives of so many writers and artists, a severe change in the open and welcoming atmosphere for American art occurred. Innovation in both style and meaning was forced to move underground, and the vitality of American writing that had made it the world leader during the twentieth century was diminished. Its invigorating energy was replaced with constraint.

One of the most apparently dangerous parts of the literary inheritance from the 1930s was political—any emphasis on collective action was considered an approval of socialism, if not Communism. As Granville Hicks had predicted, "the literary united front has disappeared . . . there has been a sharp revulsion against the Soviet Union . . . aggravated by the tangled issues of the Second World War."[2] That all promise from the proletarian movement of the 1930s was erased affected all kinds of intellectual and liberal thinking. Christopher Lasch recalls the 1950s as completely controlled and completely unplayful; he concludes that the Cold War ended any trace of "intellectual excitement" for political thought.[3]

It is certainly true that a cold-war outlook dominated American culture during the decade and more that followed the end of World War II. The known world seemed to be divided into two camps, and for many Americans those camps constituted, on one side, the forces of light—democracy, capitalism, religion—and on the other what they perceived as the forces of darkness and repression and of unknown (and therefore suspect) religion.

American responses to this bifurcation were, for the most part, restrictive. Rather than attempting to understand the other, different, cultures, people in the United States were smug about their prosperity, their winning the war, and their cultural stability. In 1950s America, there seemed to be only one good way to do anything, and people who did things in a different style, or for different ends, were suspect. Even cultural critics like Lionel Trilling argued that intellectual maturity consisted of an ability to hold contradictory ideas in tension rather than needing to commit to any single ideology.

Class in the 1940s Novel

Hicks had rightly foreseen a change in class allegiance. While much of 1930s fiction had depicted the poor, it might have been acceptable, or even fashionable, to learn about that deprived class. But what glamour in strangeness existed a decade earlier quickly evaporated in the glow of the suburbs, complete with their electric mixers, automatic washing machines, dryers, and television sets. As Hicks had predicted, "some sort of aristocratic, authoritarian doctrine is going to grow in influence among the intellectuals."[4]

From a retrospective view, Christopher Lasch saw that the many cultural changes of the 1940s resulted in a new kind of liberalism, one characterized by "its unconcealed elitism and its adulation of wealth, power, and 'style.'"[5] In this mood of an acquiring middle and upper class and a resultant upward mobility, people wanted to read about characters who were also economically successful. Unless writers could tell stories about the pastoral poor, the brave but honest class that had so long satisfied as an obligatory subject for condescension in any good Christian culture, they had best focus on narratives about stock markets, country clubs, and urban expansion.

What they did *not* want to read about was the world Nelson Algren created in his fourth novel, *The Man with the Golden Arm* (1949). Advertised as a highly sensational and sexual book, Algren's study of Chicago's not only very poor but criminal culture did not try to disguise the lives of Frankie Machine and his strangely crippled wife, Sophie, of the sycophant Sparrow Saltskin, of Captain Bednar (the policeman whose passion for control led to his nickname "Record Head"), of Antek, who owns the bar, of Drunkie John and his beautiful lover, Molly Novotny, of Louie the drug supplier, of Piggy, who ends up rich, of Umbrella Man, and of the Division Street prostitutes, junkies, and thieves.

Algren was no Sherwood Anderson, however, and his purpose in writing the book was not to create a gallery of grotesques for the reader to hold at arm's length. Algren does not use the term "degenerate" to refer to his Division Street people—that was some shocked reviewer's word. Yet another wounded World War II vet, Frankie has a number of handicaps as he tries to find a successful route through life. The biggest one is that he was born in those streets; he knows nothing but gambling, drinking, and whoring, nor does he know how to get out. Besides, the pathetic Sparrow idolizes him and has waited for his return so that they can be friends again. Unfortunately, Frankie "belongs."

When his young wife develops hysterical paralysis as a result of an automobile accident (Frankie is driving, and they have been drinking), his natural optimism, not to mention his considerable skill as a dealer, begins to fade. Facing Sophie and her obsessive jealousy takes more energy than Frankie has. Walking the tightrope between pleasing the café owner (who runs the game Frankie deals) and his regulars (who must win once in a while) takes energy as well. Trying to keep the stupidly reckless Sparrow out of jail yet another time wears on his remaining nerves. Inevitably, once the reader has come to admire this small tough man, Frankie turns—quietly—to drugs.

The Man with the Golden Arm is no sociological treatise. The character of Frankie has the reader by the heart. Although it was considerably beneath the moral and ethical level of its mainstream contemporary readers (who found the book once it won the National Book Award for Fiction), Algren's novel meant a great deal to them. But even as they recognized that Algren vividly conveys a certain life on the Chicago streets, they had to pretend to know nothing about that life (and its morality).

Algren's narrative—paced to mimic the hurried yet furtive existence of men on the run and of the women who make themselves available (day or night) for their sexual needs—is a collage of dialogue, action, and poignant monologue. Readers responded to the author's effective writing. Admitting to himself that he is in trouble over his killing Louie, as well as desperate to go off with Molly and leave the complaining Sophie, Frankie

> sat on the bed's edge and smoked a cigarette while Rumdum [the dog] nuzzled between his knees. Once the latch rattled suddenly and he wondered why he could never get used to the way the El rattled it.
> "Wheel me a little, Frankie."
> That meant she would sleep in the chair tonight, and he wheeled her till her head slipped onto her shoulder in a light doze. Beside the gas plate's feeble warmth she napped lightly, with the little blue flames playing on her nodding head; beneath the chair Rumdum shivered. The overhanging blankets kept the cold off his hide a bit down there.
> From under the heaped army blankets on the bed—blankets stolen from army camps all the way from Fort Bragg to Camp Maxey—Frankie peered out, with one limp eye, upon the new year's calendar: January 1, 1947. Outside the pane the year's first snow turned into the year's first rain.[6]

Frankie Majcinek, bearing a name Anglicized to "Machine" both for convenience and as tribute to his skilled and tireless dealing, finds within himself common decency, love, and a true self-knowledge. As Frankie mourns for the man he might have been, Algren writes, "He had never been trusted. He had never trusted himself."[7]

The waste of the mean streets Algren creates is the loss of human potential. Back on drugs, helpless to do anything but kill himself, Frankie passes quickly from the reader's sight. Algren uses the blunt but effective tactic of recording the inquest statements about Frankie's death to close the novel. In them, the poetry of the Chicago streets reverberates with the sense of Frankie Machine— and his loss.

For Harriette Arnow, poverty is a means to stability, rather than a threat. When Kentucky farmers choose to live God-fearing if meager lives, partly to stay among the Appalachian hills that provide what beauty their lives contain, they test themselves and their families in that living. But whereas Depression-era poverty was seen as potentially ennobling, 1950s prosperity regarded all poverty as degrading. Arnow's romantic portraits of Nunn Ballew, the hunter of *Hunter's Horn* (1949), his wife, Milly, and their children and neighbors give way in her second novel, *The Dollmaker* (1954), to a blend of realism and naturalism.

Reviewed as the story of a passionate maverick, *Hunter's Horn* fits one pattern of 1940s novels in that even though it was written by a woman, it has a male protagonist. For women writers at midcentury to be published, they needed to produce a traditional novel (one with a male hero, or at least protagonist). Arnow's Nunn is dominant because he represents the status of men in his culture. Whether he is fighting a roomful of men when he is crazy-drunk or selling the livestock in order to buy a pair of pedigreed hunting dogs (dooming his family to a meatless year), Nunn is above reproach. A man's sins are expected; quick and severe punishment, however, falls on women and children for their foibles.

Arnow was one of the first midcentury novelists to interrogate religious belief. A dangerous position, in part, as the reigning conservative philosophy accepted religion as one base of Americanism—but Arnow in both novels shows the hypocrisy of a community so intent on observing the forms of religion that it does not recognize its essence. In her works, characters who thrive on personal cruelty are often safe in the bosom of the Church.

Nunn's self-serving vanity is his corruption. Although he intends to be a good provider, husband, and father, once hunting season starts, he resumes his obsession with catching the larger-than-life red fox, King Devil. Driven to both exhaustion and drink by his fanaticism, Nunn remains a marginal farmer and a thoughtless, angry parent. The tragedy of *Hunter's Horn* is that as the Ballew children mature, their lives are crippled irrevocably by Nunn's failures. The irony of his name—signifying either religious dedication or its absence—is only one of the many ironies in the book.

Arnow's structure contributes to the pervasive irony. *Hunter's Horn* begins and ends with scenes in which Nunn is obviously controlling the family destiny. In the opening, Nunn is buying winter provisions for his family—yard goods, sugar, shoes, candy, and canned dog food. The positive scene melds into the reader's sure knowledge that Nunn cares less for his family than for his boast that this year he will get King Devil. Like Melville's Ahab, he rationalizes whatever will help him conquer the fox. While Nunn does not take his children on the hunts or put them in outright physical danger, he robs them of what little supplemental nourishment they might have had and clothes them too poorly to allow them to continue their schooling. He also risks his own life repeatedly while drunk. And inevitably, he keeps Milly pregnant.

The novel closes with another highly charged scene, this one of Nunn's deciding what to do about the scandal of his daughter's illicit pregnancy. By sending to Detroit for the father, the no-good Mark Cramer, and placing Suse into service as well, Nunn succumbs to social pressure and in the process destroys both Suse and her mother, Milly. For the reader who expected a bildungsroman, with Nunn learning from experience, Arnow's ending is devastating proof that his character is not redeemable. More irony derives from the fact that Nunn continues to stand high among the men of the community.

Within the framework of what seems to be Nunn's story, Arnow establishes the spheres of the women characters' lives. Much of the novel deals with women's daily life activities—their nurturing, tending the sick, mourning the dead. The true hero of the novel is Milly, a fearless, loving woman who bonds with other women, understands her children, and tries to help Nunn get through his barren life. It is also Milly who finally traps the fox.

In Arnow's *The Dollmaker*, Gertie Nevels assumes the role of protagonist in ways Milly does not. With both financial means and physical strength, Gertie challenges her society's expectations about her role as wife to a man fascinated with machinery. Clovis's need to work in the auto industry in Detroit—the same kind of obsession as Nunn's need to catch the fox—makes Gertie's reasonable plan to buy a Kentucky farm impossible. The novel follows the strong and competent farmer, Gertie, into the urban labyrinth that disorients her and kills her children. Detroit is a petty, hateful place, filled with people of different races and creeds, a site of cruel opportunism. Temporarily, Gertie's sense of self shrinks.

Prejudice, poverty, differing standards of living—the Detroit community gives Gertie a range of new experiences. At first she is reproving, but eventually she sees that women's problems are the same everywhere. Other women turn to her for comfort and strength. She falters twice—once, after her older son has run back to Kentucky, leaving his farewell note for Clovis instead of her; a second time, for a much longer period, after Cassie's brutal death on the train tracks.

Through her breakdown, however, Gertie finds a new perspective on life. The carving that she considered a hobby becomes a way of making ends meet, and she finds satisfaction in destroying the block of beautiful wood she had earlier saved to carve the face of Christ.

Finding that face among her many simple neighbors, Gertie relinquishes her need to achieve greatness. She is content to achieve sanity and income and to secure her children's lives.

Taken together, Arnow's novels present a full picture of the peaceful yet restrictive Cumberland culture, changed greatly by the intrusion of World War II, the opportunities for people to move north, and the disillusion when urban life proves to be less prosperous and less satisfying than rural. Each novel praises the person who follows his or her heart, who commits self to land and work, and who lives for the good of the family rather than selfishly. In these traits, Arnow defines what Christianity can mean to the modern world.

Wallace Stegner's Elsa, the woman whose life is charted in *The Big Rock Candy Mountain* (1943), has much in common with both Gertie and Milly. Married to Bo Mason, Elsa sees her life replicate that of her mother, who also married young and then, at 34, died a lingering death from backbreaking work on the Minnesota farm. After she died, her husband remarried—to the much younger Sarah, one of Elsa's best friends. Running from her father's infidelity, as she interprets it, Elsa travels to North Dakota to live with an uncle. The attraction of the renegade Bo, a man's man who lives the dream of quick riches in the new American West, is only partly sexual. Elsa has been displaced in her immediate family, and what she wants most of all is "a place of my own where I can sit down and everything there is mine and everything I do means something."[8]

Stegner's long novel emphasizes the futility of the American dream. Already long settled, the West has been plundered; the frontier is gone. By the time Bo reaches any territory, wealthy land developers have skimmed off whatever profits are to be had. Even his flight into Canada brings nothing, and as the family separates and then reunites, his anger over his lost dream makes him more and more violent. Stegner minces no words: Bo's tragic flaw is "his unwillingness to face the consequences of his own acts, his impatience at restraint and responsibility and the gnawing awareness that he was still responsible. He could neither accept those responsibilities nor run completely away from them."[9]

Like Ma Joad in John Steinbeck's *The Grapes of Wrath* and Gertie Nevels in *The Dollmaker*, Elsa Mason holds the family in place. She raises the two boys and tries to ameliorate their sometimes brutal conflicts with their father. (The one time she does physically leave Bo is after his vicious treatment of the children; clearly, Stegner implies, any man who behaves in such a way deserves to lose his family.) Elsa lives many years longer than her mother did, although she dies as painfully. Bruce, the younger son who has become a lawyer, the son left alive, narrates those last years and sees only the waste of his bullying father's life. When Bo kills himself and his current lover in a hotel lobby, Bruce feels little sorrow. Whatever grief his parents' lives evoked has been already spent at his mother's bedside.

The western version of the American dream is finding the "big rock candy mountain." Stegner's ironically titled chronicle of the abuse of love and personal value within the confines of the American family, built on its core premise of the patriarchy—that men provide the living and the moral strength for the family—is strangely somber. Prescient of the questioning that the American interest in existentialism was to prompt, Stegner's novel is an important text for a realistic look into the myth of the frontier, men's relation to that myth, and the demise of the family in the hard setting of poverty and want.

Poverty remains the villain in any culture that values possessions. Whether a family is moral or not, its position in a community—based on its income and the housing and food that income provides—is a primary determinant of emotional and psychic health. Works as different as these by Algren, Arnow, and Stegner all raise serious questions about economic well-being in relation to family unity and human integrity. Ann Petry's *The Street*, published as a Book of the Month Club selection in 1946, is another prism for understanding the pervasive conflict between what a character tries to achieve and the frustrating poverty that blocks even reasonable attempts to live.

Lutie Johnson's life is a series of financial shocks. When she marries and has a child, her life choices are predicated on her husband's earning a reasonable living. Their house in the suburbs is the apex of their American dream—but throughout the book, Petry is careful to enunciate how difficult attaining such a dream is for American blacks. The loss of her husband's job means that Lutie must take on the responsibility of earning; to earn enough for the mortgage payment, she must finally leave New York and take a live-in job with a white family in Connecticut. Heartbroken that she must care for this little boy instead of her own Bub, she yet believes her family will value her work.

But, predictably, being a house-husband is not enough for her spouse; and when she returns home early one evening Lutie finds him in bed with another woman. Leaving him, she moves into her father's place; then she must worry about the influences Bub is subject to in that environment. So Lutie finds the only kind of apartment she can afford, she and Bub move in, and the reader meets the inhabitants of *The Street*.

Petry's grotesques and prostitutes did not meet with quite the same reaction as Algren's did. In her novel, unlike *The Man with the Golden Arm*, the driving force is precisely Lutie's own morality. Frankie Machine succumbs to all the evils his street provides; Lutie fights desperately to stay respectable. In her case, becoming a prostitute would be the easy route, but she sees her work as nightclub singer as a legitimate second job. She does not understand that not being paid while she gets experience singing is a means to coerce her into sex with either the white club owner or Boots, the black band leader.

Along with realistic situations and writing techniques, Petry uses the authorial voice to make judgments about her characters. There is no question in the reader's mind that Lutie Johnson is doing the best she can and that the steady infiltration of corruption that infuses the novel makes the horrifying denouement—for both Lutie and Bub—all too predictable. As a work of immense power, *The Street* satisfies any reader who knows what being relentlessly poor can do to a human being. Petry establishes a situation that does not lend itself to any American dream, and as she works through inevitable act after inevitable act, the reader is drawn to finish the book through a reaction of terror rather than expectation. For the reader, as for Lutie Johnson, expectation of anything good is long since past.

The "New Fiction" of the 1940s

None of these writers—Algren, Petry, Arnow, or Stegner—wrote the new fiction of the 1940s as Chester E. Eisinger defines it. While he insists that there is, on the one hand, no such thing as a cohesive new body of work, he identifies the books cradled in that category as works of modernism (written in new ways, with craft once again privileged), with particular thematic considerations. They are not books stemming from any philosophical or social-political agenda.

He mentions novels by Paul Bowles ("desperate nihilism"), Truman Capote ("gothic decadence"), and Jean Stafford.[10]

We have seen the way the 1940s closed ranks against literary innovation once people realized that World War II meant that the voicing of any unpatriotic sentiments could kill Americans. If some part of a literary mainstream was Communist, or at least advocated communal or collective action—such as unionization—then to continue that strain of writing during the war was to promulgate conspiracy if not mutiny or espionage. We have seen, too, the way the normal war novel was a reification of male power and prowess, of heterosexuality, and of (perhaps in its very absence) the values of the American dream, family life, and religion. Setting the two strands of understandable belief in place so that they crossed, the reader could anticipate a plethora of "family values" fiction. There would be little criticism of either the country or its dream; there would be little questioning of the values that were implied in that dream.

But as we have also seen, the influence of European questioning (since Europe's world outlook, based on its very different participant role in World War II, was bleaker than that of the United States) had fed into a strand of existential fiction that puzzled readers, provoked them into thinking for themselves instead of reassuring them. (Paul Bowles's writing is important for his presentation of characters and situations that shocked establishment culture.)

A kind of perverse satisfaction with finding holes in the fabric of the American dream prompted general readers as well as students and intellectuals to read a range of fiction. What people were most interested in, probably because of the impact of existentialism on literature throughout the world, was the depiction of the loss of innocence. Resurgent sales of Hemingway's *The Sun Also Rises* and Fitzgerald's *The Great Gatsby* reflected that fascination; but the clearest testimony to the self-conscious need to question accepted national values was in the writing of a new generation of writers.

Such writers as Truman Capote, Gore Vidal, Carson McCullers, and other southerners (Peter Taylor, Eudora Welty, Elizabeth Spencer, Flannery O'Connor, Shirley Ann Grau) may have been alienated from mainstream culture because of sexual preference or agnosticism. For whatever biographical reasons, their fiction during the 1940s and the 1950s created a new category of American letters—that of the minority viewpoint (though white), the literature of the anti-dream. Expressing themselves in nonrealistic, or at least unconventionally structured, works, these newer writers insisted on the dreamlike (or, sometimes, hallucinatory) quality of much human experience. At their most ephemeral, novels by these visionary if fragile writers were written to disguise the narratives being conveyed.

Capote's *Other Voices, Other Rooms* (1948) illustrates graphically how a text can antagonize mainstream readers. In its beginning, Capote appears to be writing the Horatio Alger, boy-as-orphan tale. Joel Harrison Knox is introduced as a 13-year-old "delicate" boy, marked by "a girlish tenderness,"[11] motherless, and living with his aunt's family. His prayer as he travels to the home of his long-lost father, to the forbidding Skully's Landing, is "God, let me be loved."[12] Capote's novel is not a lost-boy text, however; it is the story of Randolph Skully, cross-dressing transvestite, who has plotted for young Joel to come to the Skully house, even though his no-good father has been paralyzed as a result of Randolph's sinister love life.

The machinations of Randolph—as well as his tawdry history—comprise the second half of the book. Its denouement, much to the horror of its readers, is that Joel decides to stay with Randolph; true to the older man's intentions, the child has been corrupted. What Capote does very well is to paint the allure of the genteel misfit's world so that it echoes the young boy's unformed desires: Randolph's room, for example, is "so unlike anything he'd [Joel] ever known before: faded gold and tarnished silk reflecting in ornate mirrors, it all made him feel as if he'd eaten too much candy."[13] Given the poor life Skully's Landing can provide, the allure of this room/this dream vision is understandable.

Other characters in the novel provide vitality: Idabel is a charming adventurer; Zoo and Little Sunshine show Joel that it is possible to live in fantasy worlds; and Dolores and Pepe Alvarez suggest the shadowy meaning of desire. But the book increasingly leaves the real world, dominated by a father whose only guidance comes from a trail of little red balls, and settles into the atmosphere of Randolph's room. Little Sunshine tries to describe the aura of mystery when he recalls "other voices, other rooms, voices lost and clouded, strummed his dreams."[14] That much of the closing action takes place in the Cloud Hotel has been, then, anticipated. When Capote writes that Joel "drifted deep into September,"[15] he signals the reader that the factual will no longer be the norm in this novel of bisexual, transsexual identities.

Other Voices, Other Rooms is much more than a book about homo-sexuality. In contrast to Gore Vidal's *The City and the Pillar*, which was published earlier in 1948, the Capote work is a deft, almost translucent piece of writing, carried by a sensuous rhythm through the filmy scenes that never quite "mean" what they seem to mean. Joel's bewilderment at having seen the woman in the upper-story window represents his confusion at the kind of family, the kind of household, Skully's Landing shelters. Rather than leaving adolescent sexual experience unspecified, as Capote does, Vidal writes a detailed scene of the sex between Joe Willard and Bob Ford. Camping out after Ford's graduation from high school, the boys' wrestling match turns into an embrace and culminates in the sex act—after which Ford makes reference to "a hell of a mess" and "awful kid stuff."[16] Vidal keeps the sex going for the rest of the weekend, however.

In rushed episodes that are meant to give the reader some insight into the amorphous nature of sexuality, Vidal loads his novel with scenes of men's avoidance of women (Ford marries the high school girlfriend he disdained because she was easy—or, perhaps, not easy). The implausible book ends with the first intimate encounter in years between the high school friends. Set up by Joe to be drunk in a hotel room they are sharing, Ford resists Joe's advances. Joe then murders him—as much for his verbal insult, the reader supposes, as for his refusal. The heavy if inept symbolism of the title (and the second section, subtitled "The Pillar of Salt"), marking Joe's discovery of and turn to homosexuality as the inevitable result of his lovemaking with Ford, clarifies little about the psychological differences between the protagonists.

Vidal tries to shade his character into some kind of complexity; the opening of the book draws on an atmosphere of mysterious confusion as Joe is described trying to drink himself into oblivion. He has already killed Ford: "The moment was strange. There was no reality in the bar; there was no longer solidity; all things merged. . . ."[17] Less a description of intriguing personality than one of drunkenness, this scene is also filled with false narrative clues. Joe mourns, it seems, for a time when "a certain person had been with him";[18] yet according to the plot about to unfold, Bob Ford had been with Joe only once—years before. What Vidal's book does successfully is provide the reader who is uninformed about homosexuality with a set of descriptions of gay bars, approaches, and the physical accouterments of life within queer culture.

These works by Vidal and Capote were more at variance with the mainstream culture of the late 1940s and the 1950s to come than they would have been with the avant-garde America of the 1920s and the 1930s because, as John Updike phrased it recently, "The '50s should be understood as . . . a postwar decade—with something prim and spartan about it, a kind of platoon discipline in its swiftly assembled families. The returning veterans had set the tone . . . serious study, leading to the private redoubt of the career, the kids, the collie and the tract house."[19] Whatever one undertook in postwar America, it should be serious. It should also, with the insistent emphasis on families, be heterosexual.

Carson McCuller's *The Heart Is a Lonely Hunter* (1940) was greeted with praise not so much because it tested the boundaries of normal portrayals of sexuality but because it treated with dignity and love a group of people—classic misfits, all—who were related only through human sympathy. In both Biff Brannon's New York Cafe and Mick Kelly's boardinghouse home, the strange wanderers of McCuller's first novel make their connections.

At their center sits Mister Singer, a boarder at Kelly's who eats his meals at the New York Cafe. This wise deaf-mute mourns his love for his deaf-mute friend, Spiros Antonapoulos, a Greek who had been institutionalized by his cousin after he had lived with Singer for many years. Singer visits Antonapoulos whenever he has vacation time; the rest of his days he goes to work and then listens well to anyone who speaks to him. He can, of course, hear nothing, but his expression is so sympathetic that he becomes a confidante for adults and adolescents like Mick; whites and blacks like Dr. Copeland.

The labyrinth of relationships winds slowly through the southern village before being jarred suddenly by Mick's sexual act with the neighbor boy and even more suddenly by Singer's suicide in his boardinghouse bedroom. Bereft after his return from his attempt to visit Antonapoulos (who had died), Singer shoots himself as placidly as he had accepted the weight of his acquaintances' tragedies. Another of the characters leaves town rather than be charged with the murder of a black man; Biff's wife dies suddenly, and he finds himself thinking of Mick; and Mick grows up and takes a job at Woolworth's to help the family survive economically. Her story will continue in McCullers's 1946 *The Member of the Wedding*.

As she does in her 1941 novella, *Reflections in a Golden Eye,* McCullers writes with a fluid objectivity that makes the aberrations of her grotesque characters seem normal. Here the assumed sexual deviance is more flamboyant: a captain with decided homosexual tendencies watches the progress of his wife's affair with a major. When he rides his wife's horse, Firebird, and then beats the animal, he takes part in a self-punishment that echoes his confusion over his shame in being impotent with his wife and recognizing his ardor for the major.

Captain Penderton is described early in terms of his sexuality: "He stood in a somewhat curious relation to the three fundaments of existence—life itself, sex, and death. Sexually the Captain obtained within himself a delicate balance between the male and female elements, with the susceptibilities of both the sexes and the active powers of neither."[20] It is Penderton's trying to find a way to take action that provides the plot of the book.

McCullers complicates the narrative by focusing on a character seemingly outside the action: Private Williams, the young soldier who cares for Firebird, who lusts after Mrs. Penderton (to the extent that he watches nights at her bedside), and who likes to run and ride nude on the base. A plethora of other people on the military base add to the complications, among them Major Morris Langdon's dying wife, Alison, and her attentive Filipino houseboy, Anacleton. It is Alison's premonition about the skulking Williams outside the Penderton house that leads to the community's discovery of his vigils at Leonora Penderton's bedside: by this time, however, Captain Penderton is obsessively in love with the young soldier and so takes no action. It is also in a conversation between Alison and Anacleton that the title image occurs. Anacleton, an amateur painter, tries to describe a vision he has of

"A peacock of a sort of ghastly green. With one immense golden eye. And in it these reflections of something tiny and—"
In his effort to find just the right word he held up his hand with the thumb and forefinger touched together. His hand made a great shadow on the wall behind him. "Tiny and—
"Grotesque," she [Alison] finished for him.[21]

Immediately after confronting Anacleton's grotesque image of a pervasive evil, Alison has the first of the serious heart attacks that soon end her life. McCullers had previously drawn her as a woman deranged by the slow death of her only child and by her husband's careless affairs. Like Mister Singer in the earlier book, Alison becomes a kind of receptacle for the knowledge of inhuman, as well as human, misery.

The narrative action that occurs, finally, is that Penderton kills both Williams and himself on the night he finds the younger man once more beside Leonora's bed. The last quarter of *Reflections in a Golden Eye* traces the upright captain's dangerously visible passion for the seemingly unaware young man: it is an almost parodic replica of heterosexual courtship, even more unexpected in that it is set on a military base.

> He was in a constant state of repressed agitation. His preoccupation with the soldier grew in him like a disease. As in cancer, when the cells unaccountably rebel and begin the insidious self-multiplication that will ultimately destroy the body, so in his mind did the thoughts of the soldier grow out of all proportion to their normal sphere. Sometimes with dismay he made a wondering resume of the steps that had brought about this condition. . . . How his annoyance could have grown to hate, and the hate to this diseased obsession, the Captain could not logically understand.
>
> A peculiar reverie had taken hold of him. . . .[22]

Anticipating the interest in psychological states of mind, McCullers created a fiction that was fascinating in its attention to the enigmatic, the unexplained character.

She also builds into the narrative information to fill the obvious narrative gaps—that Williams has murdered a man five years earlier, that Penderton is subject to trance states in which he acts without preparation (or reason), that most of these characters seem to see the sex act as more animal response than emotional. But her second novel, like *The Heart Is a Lonely Hunter*, presents such characters without apology. The kind of objective distance she achieves as she recounts these aberrant behaviors sets her fiction apart from anything written during the 1930s or early 1940s. John Aldridge links her with Truman Capote, about whose characters the critic writes that they serve no moral purpose at all but exist "simply to evoke in us feelings of horror, perhaps to fascinate us momentarily with the ingenuity of their grotesqueness."[23]

McCullers's fiction does more. By drawing such characters as Mick, Williams, Mister Singer, Alison, and Biff with a kindly eye, she invites the reader's understanding of the innate differences in people and their responses. By emphasizing the lack of choice of her economically disadvantaged characters, she becomes a naturalistic writer and has more in common with the novelists of the 1930s than might be readily apparent. But because these characters tend to be bisexual, or amorphous enough that readers could be uncomfortable with their sexual preferences, critics categorized McCullers as a new kind of writer, one whose characters were more unlike those of other American novels than they were like them. In the reviews as in the works, the text of sexuality is hazy, seldom specified, almost ignored. It served the literary community well to have the classification of "new fiction" to help disguise some of these directions.

What happened during the 1940s is that the antagonisms of the middle-class reader came into full play. Reading about the poor was acceptable as long as there were no calls to action, no prolegomena for change, embedded in the text. Nostalgia for the days of parents' or grandparents' hard times was not only a reasonable mode; it fit in well with the premises of the American dream. Having benefited from years of struggle and education, children were supposed to do better financially than their ancestors had. As it had been during the Depression, the class of characters portrayed became a determinant of what books a person chose to read.

Of even greater significance was the way an author drew the lives of the poor. Reading about objectionable behaviors—whether or not they could be traced to lives of want and need—did not fit into a middle-class mindset. The risk of finding Frankie Machine or Molly Novotny memorable was itself threatening: therefore, nice people did not admit to reading Algren. The danger of finding Randolph Skully's transvestitism interesting from even a sociological perspective warned those same nice readers away from Truman Capote, Gore Vidal, and, somewhat earlier, Carson McCullers. Without any conscious design, books that upheld the status quo—which was growing increasingly conservative and more formally religious—sold better. During the autumn of 1948, for example, the lead speaker for the American Book Association and New York *Herald Tribune* Book and Author Luncheon was General Dwight D. Eisenhower.

One avenue of merchandising that kept books by Algren, Farrell, Arnow, and Petry on the shelves was an emphasis on their definition as "other." The lives of degradation about which they wrote belonged to people who were different from "real" Americans—besides being poor, these characters were often immigrants, black, or rural. As long as authors wrote about outsiders, their books might hold some kind of anthropological interest. And to make room for the innovative fiction being written about white characters in the States—as in the work of Capote, McCullers, Welty, and Grau—reviewers and booksellers created a new category, the southern novel. Thus taught to regard the South as far removed from the typical, prosperous landscapes of American life, readers learned to find even the white characters in southern fictions as exotic, weird, and strange as the characters found in gothic literature.

5

Publishers' Dreams and Nightmares

Choices about what appeared in print during the 1950s continued to be profit driven. Like other segments of the economy, publishing expected to be flooded with best-sellers once Americans' pent-up war savings could be spent; the problem for publishers was to determine what kinds of books consumers would buy.

An increasing, if small, interest in the work of black writers was fueled partly by some older editors' and publishers' recalling the Harlem and Chicago renaissances in the 1920s. More of it, however, resulted from the fact that Ann Petry's first novel, *The Street*, had sold a million copies. The truth is that in publishing circles as in the general culture there was no category labeled *black writing* (or Negro writing). Nor was there any suggestion that the designation *writing by people of color* would come to dominate certain areas of the marketplace in another 30 years.

Issues of Race in Fiction

By the 1950s, older definitions of social norms based upon race and ethnicity were, after years of liberal attack, finally falling. In 1954 the Supreme Court agreed that separate education for black and white students gave minorities *un*equal opportunity, rather than equal, and so abrogated any legal defense of segregation. In 1955, Rosa Parks—by not giving her seat near the front of a bus to a white person—refused to accept the concept of black inferiority. Her arrest set the stage for the Montgomery, Alabama, bus boycott and the rise of the young black minister Martin Luther King Jr. to national prominence. These and other episodes of resistance produced deep cultural change. What happened in contemporary literary theory as a result of cultural change was a redefinition of "minority" writing.

Movements for cultural change created the idea of black pride and thus generated a new consciousness about history and art among people who had previously been marginalized. Writers of color and women both of color and of white skins increasingly responded to the need to speak for themselves, in their own distinctive voices. Locating their publishing centers in cities often remote from New York, Boston, and Los Angeles (the usual places influential journals and reviews begin), they made prominent Detroit, San Francisco, Houston, Albuquerque, and Atlanta. The Black Arts movement, El Teatre Campesino, dozens of new magazines and festivals—all represent significant moments in the development of alternative cultural and publication centers.

But in the 1940s and the 1950s, black writers were few enough that they could publish within the usual channels—indeed, their very existence depended on being accepted in those established channels. In literary histories of these decades, black writers are usually categorized—when they are mentioned—as naturalists, and there is hardly any discussion of their writing as a racial unity. We have seen the way Ann Petry's *The Street* satisfied demand for a realistic portrayal of poverty and degradation and their impact upon the core of black family life. Powerful as that novel was, it was a repetition in many ways of Richard Wright's *Native Son*. Lutie Johnson has few choices after she kills Boots. To abandon her child to grow up in a house of correction, while being terribly at the mercy of the careless streets, is obviously not a genuine choice. In Petry's novel, economic wherewithal remains everything: Boots, like Lutie, cannot afford to offend people with money. Wealth obscures human loyalty and color lines. When Boots is ordered to give Lutie to his white employer, the issue of Lutie's race (in contrast to the whiteness of his boss) does not enter his limited mind.

It was the genius of Ralph Ellison's unnamed but very definitely black "invisible man" to cross both economic and racial lines. Long a student of the American and European modernists, Ellison plays with most of the conventions of twentieth-century fiction while yet adhering to many distinctly black narrative, musical, and oral traditions. The book, published to great acclaim in 1952, gives the reader a central protagonist, but never names or describes him. To refer to the character, then, readers must keep repeating the thematic tag, "invisible man." Not only a person without a country—though he is also that—Ellison's character is a man without a body, without a presence, adrift from all human community. He exists as he does entirely through subterfuge and self-created energy. The invisible man's "success" within the upwardly mobile American culture is that he manages to live in his own space, literally carved out of someone else's property and then suitably illuminated with stolen electric power.

The child of Faulkner and Hemingway as well as Wright, Gwendolyn Brooks, and Langston Hughes, Ellison composed an elegantly complex narrative score as carefully and yet—witness the many dizzying riffs—as improvisationally as might have the jazz musician he had once studied to become. The solid block structure of a conventional bildungsroman is here cut into and underscored with humorous asides, scenes, and dialogue that keeps the reader from any complacency—or from feeling that any event in the novel is predictable. As quixotic as most human life felt itself to be in the post–atomic bomb milieu, "invisible man" became a touchstone character for many readers.

And that was, in part, Ellison's gift at that moment in time—to give readers a black character who was no blacker than they. Critics of today have traced the author's countless uses of jazz, black idiom, black foods, and black customs throughout the novel; but reading it in 1952—without benefit of critical commentary—was a very human if unscholarly experience. The pain of being invisible, the pain of knowing that everyone in your experience is ready to betray you, the pain of wondering where you would find a safe harbor (once you could determine what your personality and/or sexuality consisted of): the themes of *Invisible Man* are the themes of emergent adolescence and young adulthood, regardless of race or culture. As J. D. Salinger had already discerned through readers' responses to his *New Yorker* stories, postwar Americans were caught in a perpetual adolescence. Unsure about why the Allies had won the war, unsure that the vaunted privileges of the middle class were really desirable, unsure that the consumerism that drove the postwar decade was healthy, war survivors (women as well as men) went back in time to revisit their determining years. Less prosperous, those years were perhaps, somehow, better. Novels that explored themes of interest to those questioning, self-conscious minds were earnestly read and discussed, even if they were written by writers of a different color or ethnicity.

That Ellison was black created a double-bind situation. For some, his blackness seemed exotic; for others, black fiction meant sociology or worse—something to be read with patronage or condescension. That attitude can be seen in the *Publishers' Weekly* announcement of the novel, where it is described as "[a] bitter, occasionally brilliant book of a black boy's progress from the South to Harlem."[1] The fact that Ellison saw no real "progress" for his invisible man and that he had tried to avoid writing the "black boy" narrative had no impact on the anonymous critic. But "brilliant" the book is, and readers respond to its unusual rhythms, its superlatively complex sentences.

As Laura Doyle has recently pointed out, however, no one is ever "race-neutral," either white writers or black.[2] She sees the "interruptive narrative" of *Invisible Man* as an example of Ellison's awareness of such differences: "the racial elements of the one tradition (strategically implicit in white tradition and strategically explicit in black) depend on the presence of the other."[3] Elements from black narrative that dominate the structure of *Invisible Man* interrupt and, in some ways, splice onto those of what the reader might consider white narrative. The result of reading the novel is that the expected "masculinized, race-bounded art" (a novel about a male character, written by a heterosexual male intellectual) is broadened to include scenes and discussions that might not otherwise have been there at all. White readers, it follows, could find more reason to identify with the unnamed protagonist than they might have found to identify with Wright's Bigger from *Native Son,* a character caught in a text that was most specifically masculinized and race-bounded.

James Baldwin sought similar acclaim as Ellison received for *Invisible Man,* but he also wanted to write a homosexual story. The young New York writer knew that telling the story of men in love was to commit both artistic and racial suicide. Discovered through his first novel, *Go Tell It on the Mountain* (1953), a predictably intense black fiction about a father-son conflict resolved through the church, Baldwin made it known that he was a serious artist. His lyrical prose was spun out of Wright's powerful realism yet mellowed with techniques drawn from memoir; it suggests the sense of a vanished and therefore less threatening time. It was clear that Baldwin was going to demand that his culture realize the tragedies inherent in its racism—his problem was how to do that when he also wanted to compete for the kind of popular success Ann Petry had known.

Like Petry's later novels and work by William Attaway, Zora Neale Hurston, Willard Motley, Richard Wright, and other black writers, Baldwin wrote about white characters. *Giovanni's Room* (1956) recounts the bittersweet narrative of a sophisticated American man surprised that he loves the Italian homosexual Giovanni with whom he lives in Paris. When David's fiancée, Hella, returns from Spain and David ends his affair with him, Giovanni is distraught. Out of work and impoverished, alone in the city, Giovanni is coerced into sexual acts with the bar owner he despises. He then murders that man, his previous benefactor.

Characteristic of the time, Baldwin does not describe Giovanni and David's lovemaking. The metaphor he uses for David's reluctance to admit his love for Giovanni is that of the title. In the room where Giovanni lives and stores his tawdry possessions, the smell of his body overcomes the tidy American. Crowded, hot, and stained with the residue of a brutal life, Giovanni's room is what David thinks he must escape. In fact, what he attempts to escape is his love for another man, the experience that has changed his life irrevocably.

Giovanni's Room is a kind of anti-American narrative as well. Baldwin suggests that the more natural elements of passion and human caring can be equated with a Mediterranean culture rather than that of the sanitized and upwardly mobile United States; he uses the contrast between national characters to replace the contrast between races. When David complains that they should leave the crowded room, Giovanni reminds him, "Forgive me, *mon cher Americain,* but Paris is not like New York, it is not full of palaces for boys like me. Do you think I should be living in Versailles instead?"[4] Later, suffused with grief over losing David, Giovanni tells him ironically, "Americans have no sense of doom, none whatever. They do not recognize doom when they see it."[5] As Baldwin's narrative makes clear, David (who lives on an allowance from his father) refuses to see that the situation, complicated as it is by Giovanni's having lost his job, will not resolve itself.

Blind to what life really is, David admits that he keeps all passion at arm's length: "Something had broken in me to make me so cold and so perfectly still and far away."[6] In contrast, after he leaves Giovanni without explanation to meet Hella at the station and his lover finds him after a three-day search, Giovanni speaks in a voice "thick with fury and relief and unshed tears":

"Where have you been?" he cried. "I thought you were dead! I thought you had been knocked down by a car or thrown into the river—what have you been doing all these days?"[7]

David's withdrawn amusement in the face of Giovanni's raw fear strikes the reader as inhumane, even perfidious. And the contrast in the emotional composition of the two lovers points toward the disastrous ending.

For Richard Wright, using a white insurance executive as the protagonist of his 1954 novel *Savage Holiday* allows him to describe a classic case of Freudian frustration. The issue of race has no part in his case-study approach: no reader can say that Erskine Fowler, forced by management to retire early from Longevity Life Insurance, has been victimized by his race. Tall, white, prosperous, Erskine has had only advantages. The plot of the novel, however, is that he has had no control over his childhood; the unmarried man has been marred psychologically by his mother's indiscriminate sexuality, by her earning her living through prostitution. Until his retirement, Fowler, a workaholic, buried his shame under a facade of middle-class prosperity. The first third of the narrative leaves the reader wondering what the point of the novel is, as Erskine tends to bore rather than interest—until he, nude from a night's sleep, locks himself out of his New York apartment when he goes into the hall for the Sunday paper.

The implausible plot weakens the novel from the start. Even if Fowler as exposed naked body serves the metaphoric purpose of showing how false his facade of self has been, the truth of the novel is that Fowler, naked man, is still Fowler, tall, middle-class white man: his crazy machinations to hide his nude body are so exaggerated that the reader has to believe he is severely deranged. What follows—the death of the five-year-old Tony Blake and his bereaved mother's willingness to be involved sexually with Fowler—continues the implausibility. Neither in the 1950s nor today are middle-class white children allowed to play without supervision on dangerous balconies of high-rise apartments. True to his obvious narrative skills, however, Wright's telling of the story is expert and borrows a number of devices from the detective genre. Complete with a fast-paced tale, sex, and Fowler's manic behavior, *Savage Holiday* is an ironic statement on the kinds of psychological damage white people can bear. That Fowler stops hiding his knowledge of sexual evil is what leads to his murder of Tony's mother. The brutality of this killing is a further ironic reference to the word *savage*. Who *are* the savages in this culture, Wright's title asks.

While the narrative similarities between the way Wright tells Fowler's story and the structure of the Bigger Thomas story in *Native Son* are clear, the kind of detailed authenticity that make the 1940 work so compelling is missing. A better choice of a work that continues to show Wright's ability is his 1945 autobiography, *Black Boy*, the last book he published before moving permanently to France. In *Black Boy*, the poignancy of a life almost deprived of its promise comes through vividly, and the reaffirmation of the need to tell the black story shapes the narrative with brilliant intensity. Truncated as the text was so that it could be published in the race-sensitive United States of 1945 (it has since been published in its entirety), it remained an evocative book with an impact that helped to shape the cultural changes to come.

Those black writers working outside any racially explicit category of necessity tapped into what appeared to be profitable segments of the mainstream marketplace. Willard Motley's *Knock on Any Door* (1947) and *Let No Man Write My Epitaph* (1958) drew from the suspense genre; Chester Himes, after writing a successful novel about black workers in California shipyards during World War II (*If He Hollers Let Him Go*, 1945*), eventually turned to a series of murder mysteries set in Harlem, with detectives "Coffin" Ed Jones and "Grave Digger" Johnson. Encouraged once he had moved to Europe by the French publisher Marcel Duhamel, Himes published *For Love of Imabelle* (1957; in 1965 retitled *A Rage in Harlem*); *The Crazy Kill* (1959); *Cotton Comes to Harlem* (1965); and others.

Frank Yerby, a popular Georgia novelist who also lived abroad, only rarely wrote about racial bigotry and prejudice (his stories "Health Card" in 1944 and "The Homecoming" in 1946 and his 1971 novel, *The Dahomean*). The author of more than 30 books, Yerby saw his purpose as entertaining a reading public. From 1947, when *The Foxes of Harrow* was a best-seller, through other historical novels such as *The Vixens* (1947), *The Golden Hawk* (1948), *Pride's Castle* (1949), *A Woman Called Fancy* (1951), and *The Saracen Blade* (1952)

*See my *Modern American Novel, 1914–1945* for discussion.

on into the 1980s, Yerby lived well on his commercially successful works.

It is sometimes said that serious black writers during this immediate postwar period were at their best writing memoir—but it
could be that reader interest was prompted by a sociological inquiry
that the genre satisfied. To read black writers was to try to learn
about their culture, their otherness. Few black writers were published without his or her audience knowing what race the writer
belonged to.

The work of Gwendolyn Brooks, whose early books are poem
collections (*A Street in Bronzeville*, 1945, and *Annie Allen*, the Pulitzer
Prize winner for 1950), was an acceptable choice for readers who
took their art with a serious dose of liberal interest. In her Chicago
poems, the reader could find enough black culture and black story
to fill several kinds of information gaps. By 1953, the year of her
novel, *Maud Martha*, Brooks had created a prose-poem style useful
for both memoir and fiction. Through counterpoint and juxtaposition, Brooks tells the story—dramatic and yet daily—of a black
woman's life, setting image against image, event against event,
withholding the self-conscious insight of the protagonist. The fragmented segments of the *Maud Martha* narrative were reviewed as a
new kind of fiction, a departure from the blunt realism of Richard
Wright and Ann Petry; the novel's impact on the fiction of other
African American women writers was to be clearly visible 30 years
later in the work of Ntozake Shange, Alice Walker, and Gloria Nay-
lor. Other than Brooks, the only comparatively well-published
black women writers at midcentury were Lorraine Hansberry,
whose *A Raisin in the Sun* (1959) was the first production by a contemporary black playwright to appear on Broadway, and Paule
Marshall, whose novel *Brown Girl, Brownstones* was also published
in 1959.

While publishers were sometimes willing to risk publishing work
by racial minorities, the almost complete indifference to Asian-
American John Okada's *No-No Boy* in 1957 was as chilling as the
good sales of Petry's *The Street* a decade before had been encouraging. Lin Yutang's novels (even *Chinatown Family* in 1948) did not
sell. Just as the writing of Filipino Carlos Bulosan had been important during World War II only to be forgotten by the 1950s, so books
by aspiring writers of color were generally overlooked until the late
1960s and 1970s.

The Popular Novel at Midcentury

Any discussion of the difference between serious literature and popular literature draws largely from ad hominem arguments about the moral worth of reading, what texts will last, and why readers read—all large categories of discussion. A more pragmatic view might be that the popular novel, in any period, is one that sells without first being taught in the academic classroom. Readers somehow discover Margaret Mitchell's *Gone with the Wind*, due in no small part to the movie's popularity; they discover F. Scott Fitzgerald's *Tender Is the Night* only after introduction-to-fiction courses.

Many popular novels are genre books—historical novels, mysteries, detective novels, romances, adventure stories. Readers assume familiarity with one such book because they have read other books that work in the same way: in the romance, handsome man loves virginal girl, but he must prove himself (and remain pure) as he tries to seduce/marry her.[8] Other popular books are so completely in tune with the times, or with the changes occurring in those times, that their appeal is irresistible. Elizabeth Long defines the popular novel as a complex phenomenon, its sales dependent on both marketing and the culture that surrounds it. It usually appeals to a broad readership, not just a subset of readers, and does so because the author shares his or her readers' perceptions of the world.[9]

Long assesses the common themes of the popular novel from World War II through the 1970s as being about success and its configuration as part and parcel of the American dream. Novels that were best-sellers immediately after the war posited the belief that an individual could find happiness as a part of corporate life (Sloan Wilson's *The Man in the Gray Flannel Suit*, 1955). Then, people wrote what Long terms the "corporate-suburban" novel, in which "work and family-centered leisure are seen as conflicting priorities" (Herman Wouk's *Marjorie Morningstar*, 1955, or Mary Ellen Chase's *The Lovely Ambition*, 1960). By the late 1960s, the contemporary popular novel suggests, people have had to define success for themselves, and the concept may have become less materialistic and more personally satisfying.[10]

Throughout these midcentury years, however, the ranks of the popular novel included about the same percentage of bodice-ripper romances (capped by Grace Metalious's phenomenally selling *Pey-*

ton Place in 1956), adventure novels that focus on the rich (from Frances Parkinson Keyes's *Came a Cavalier* in 1950 and Cameron Hawley's *Cash McCall* in 1955 to Robert Ruark's *Something of Value* in 1955 and Arthur Hailey's *Hotel* in 1965), and historical romances such as Thomas Costain's *The Moneyman* (1947), James Michener's *Hawaii* (1959), and Harold Robbins's *The Carpetbaggers* (1961).

Long points out that the mix of popular and serious novels on weekly best-seller lists remains about the same over these three decades, although it seems apparent that books by Dos Passos and Faulkner sold only to limited markets. Even Steinbeck and Hemingway had to envy best-selling novelists like A. J. Cronin, Taylor Caldwell, John P. Marquand, Shalom Asch, and Anya Seton. There are always many more popular novels than serious ones, and for some weeks, the 1990s reader will recognize not a single name from the list of fiction best-sellers.

What does change in the listing of books sold is the proportion of fiction to nonfiction books, many of which become best-sellers: the midcentury reader is clearly interested in Dale Carnegie's *How to Stop Worrying and Start Living* and the Kinsey report, *Sexual Behavior in the Human Male*. The numbers of memoirs, how-to books, etiquette guides, inspirational books, and biographies (Catherine Marshall's 1952 *A Man Called Peter* stayed on the best-seller list for years) increased with each year, and the number of fiction titles dropped off accordingly.

Other novels are made into best-sellers by readers who look for certain kinds of themes—Christian figuration, as in Lloyd C. Douglas's *The Robe* (1942) and *The Big Fisherman* (1947) and LeGette Blythe's *Bold Galilean* (1948); alternate belief systems, as in Ayn Rand's *Atlas Shrugged* (1957); exciting geographic settings, and people commensurate with them, as in Edna Ferber's *Giant* (1952) and *Ice Palace* (1958), Daphne du Maurier's *My Cousin, Rachel* (1952), and most of James Michener's work; Laura Z. Hobson's moralizing *Gentlemen's Agreement* (1947).

The arbitrariness of classification into "popular" starts to become apparent when a writer who had previously been considered "serious" and "intellectual" makes the best-seller list. Mary McCarthy made money from her 1963 *The Group* (an exposé of the lives of a group of college women), even though it rehearses a number of characters and themes from her first story collection, *The Company She Keeps* (1942), which was thought in the aftermath of the Depression to be too intellectual to be a good read. She was sometimes considered "un-American" as she satirically probed the behavior of her middle- and upper-class characters; critical of what he calls her "disengagement" and her almost clinical interest in sex, Chester E. Eisinger sees McCarthy as a writer almost too unpleasant to be read.[11]

The same kind of categorization dilemma occurs when the whole range of "war novels" is considered "popular." From the war narratives we have already discussed, such important writers of the second half of the century as Norman Mailer, Kurt Vonnegut Jr., Joseph Heller, John Hersey, Ken Kesey, and Tim O'Brien were to come. The war novel was under heavy attack from the late 1940s on when *Life* magazine used Mailer's *The Naked and the Dead* to illustrate the depravity of current American writing. Calling instead for books that portray the wide variety of American life, "the normal and decent as well as the confused and demoralized," *Life* states bluntly: "We need a novelist to recreate American values instead of wallowing in the literary slums." War novels are also considered guilty of overemphasizing disillusionment. What the American reader wants, *Life* continues, is an uplifting read.[12]

As if in response to this antipathy to the sordidly (or sensually) realistic, Betty Smith's 1948 *Tomorrow Will Be Better* led the bestseller list for some weeks. Smith's first novel (her 1943 *A Tree Grows in Brooklyn*) follows the Alger-like life of Francie Nolan as she discovers what being Irish-American and female means in the New York streets. Like many novels by ethnic or racial minorities, Smith's placed a premium on both formal education and women's self-actualization. The gentle self-discovery of both these novels' women protagonists was a change from the emphatically sexual discoveries of the heroines of 1940s and 1950s romances, and their best-sellerdom proved that readers could be discriminating in their choices of women's novels.

People who buy popular books do not care what literary critics think of their choices. They want the reassurance that their way of viewing life, relationships, religion, and the other components of normal existence is still OK. After World War II, America became even more self-conscious, and serious American literature grew more and more introspective. Both World War II and the Korean conflict became the background for a number of novels, circumstances that insured that most books would continue to have male protagonists, male narrators, and male-defined action. For readers interested in women characters (most of women readers and some men), the kind of fiction that remained open to them was the always-denigrated romance, the low-brow reading that was obtainable in any public library, bookstore, or bus stop.

Women's Writing at Midcentury

It seems particularly difficult for critics to distinguish between popular writing and serious writing when the writers concerned are women. Some criticism of American literature at midcentury, in fact, fails to mention the work of women writers at all.

Much of the most influential writing of the period, in fact, especially that which questions the norms put in place by the war novel, was the product of such women writers as Flannery O'Connor, Shirley Jackson, and Jean Stafford. One critic points out that, during the 1950s, the decade of the family, O'Connor did not write about "multigenerational households and fragmented families" but, instead, wrote austerely ironic stories of "grandparents rearing a second generation of offspring just as poorly as they had reared the first, widows supporting ungrateful adult children, single fathers neglecting their children, parents completely ignoring children because of their own self-absorption, or couples not wanting children at all."[13] How did these bleak themes create "the humor that emerges from these stories despite the tragedy or pathos of their plots?"[14]

Like the work of Flannery O'Connor, much writing by other women during the 1940s and the 1950s falls into the easy category of southern gothic. Prompted by their almost awed response to Carson McCullers's novels early in the forties, critics were glad to have some rubric, even if it were based on location, to use when writing about women's works. Not only is style in this fiction different from that of contemporary fiction by men, but the whole cast of narrative is much more internalized, much less specific in terms of the outer world and much more specific in interiority. Poemlike, much fiction by women at midcentury is so carefully crafted that few readers can discern how its technical effects are created. Critics do not use the term "workmanlike" because the seams of this writing never show. Yet almost universally, contemporary critical reaction was the same—positive, surprised, interested.

The themes of this fiction by women are seldom predictable. McCullers's writing shows the country at war, but much contemporary work by women is not "postwar." The war scarcely appears—it is seldom an influence on the lives of characters or a contributor to what happens in the plot. Situations are strangely timeless; perhaps their being set in the least productive part of the country helps to explain the nonchronological sense of event. If one old man could kill his granddaughter beside a stream in a family contest over strong-willed behavior, then another might do the same terrible thing—but whether this macabre incident happens in 1920 or 1950 seems immaterial.

It might be said that from 1940 to 1967 the world of serious women's fiction belonged to the southern school of writing, whether or not that includes the subcategory of "gothic." (Both Flannery O'Connor and Carson McCullers died young, O'Connor in 1964 and McCullers in 1967, providing a kind of ceiling to the height of critics' reliance on the term.) The use of the category "gothic" was a way to both sound learned and yet raise eyebrows over the apparent unsuitability of any woman's writing about the topics of incest, family hatred, characters' preferring pain to pleasure, and homosexual or bisexual behavior. These age-old topics originally appeared in narratives of ghosts and spirits. Eighteenth-century England enjoyed embroideries on basic horror plots, and in nineteenth-century America Edgar Allan Poe initiated the southern gothic with his exploratory narratives. More recently, William Faulkner borrowed that category to disguise some of his own potboiler aims. When modern women writers used conventions that might be linked to the gothic to describe unhealthy relationships or bizarre characters, critics were happy to note the similarity; otherwise they would have had to admit that writing by a woman as gifted as Flannery O'Connor was simply so unique that categorization was impossible.

Carson McCullers provided the literary world with more of that unique fiction, but in 1940 and 1941, when her first two books appeared, she was more readily linked with men, often with men who wrote about homosexuality. The sensual nuances of McCullers's fiction bothered her readers enough—it was often the reason they were attracted to her writing—that finding explanations within any realm of writing by women seemed unlikely. (Although the 1930s fiction of two expatriate women writers—Djuna Barnes and Anaïs Nin—influenced McCullers to write about sexual themes, most readers in the States happily ignored their work; it was the fiction of Nin's friend Henry Miller that among sexually explicit fiction first found an [underground] home in this country.)

It was easier to link McCullers with Caroline Gordon, a woman writer who had published during the 1930s and would continue writing for the next three decades. Another southerner, Gordon made her mark on the literary world with family chronicles (*Penhally*, 1931; *Aleck Maury, Sportsman*, 1934; *Green Centuries*, 1941). Acceptable because she focused these stories on male rather than female characters, Gordon experimented with narratives of women's lives in *The Women on the Porch* (1944). In general, however, she wrote well-crafted, solid narratives that were historically based (*None Shall Look Back*, 1937, a Civil War novel) and male-centered. Married for some years to Allen Tate, Gordon's reputation was secure; she provided an anchor for the whole category of southern women's writing.

Historically, the category of southern fiction written by women was linked inextricably with Ellen Glasgow. While Glasgow had begun publishing before the twentieth century, she continued to have success—and wide readership—into the 1940s. During the late 1920s and the 1930s, her novels were Book of the Month Club and Literary Guild selections, and most were best-sellers. In 1942 one of her last books, *In This Our Life*, both won the Pulitzer Prize for Fiction and was made into a popular film starring Bette Davis. In 1943 the prefaces she had written for the republication of some of her novels appeared as *A Certain Measure: An Interpretation of Prose Fiction*. Glasgow lived only until 1945; her autobiography, *The Woman Within*, was published posthumously. She remained a presence throughout midcentury.

So, too, did Gertrude Stein. Although Stein had lived abroad since 1907, her triumphant return tour during 1934 and 1935 following the publication of *The Autobiography of Alice B. Toklas* and her avant-garde opera, *Four Saints in Three Acts*, had made her nearly a household name. Lecturing throughout the States, Stein emphasized her American identity—not only in California but in Baltimore, where her family's roots ran deep. In 1940, her books *Paris France* and *What Are Masterpieces* appeared; in 1941, *Ida, A Novel*. In 1945, to much publicity as one of the most famous "liberated" Americans in France, and a Jewish woman at that, Stein promoted the third volume of her memoirs, fittingly titled *Wars I Have Seen*. An omnibus volume of her writing and her American G.I. war novel, *Brewsie and Willie*, appeared in 1946, the year she died. With her photo appearing on the cover of *Publishers' Weekly*, Stein had become one of the country's most famous women writers.

The rubric *southern* was also useful for Eudora Welty, though she was less often described as "gothic." When Welty's short stories began appearing in the late 1930s, readers throughout the country took notice. Her first story collection, *A Curtain of Green*, appeared in 1941, and its thematic emphasis on characters who live in isolation (whatever its cause) moved reviewers to compare her with McCullers and with Faulkner. Her birth in Mississippi furthered such regional comparisons—it did not seem to matter that her college degrees were from the University of Wisconsin and Columbia, that she had worked for the WPA in Chicago, and that her parents were more Midwestern than southern. By 1943, with *The Wide Net* collection, her fate as a southern writer was sealed, partly because her fiction was set either in the South or in some amorphous and seemingly primordial—or at least amoral—place that eastern critics liked to think was more kin to the South than to some place closer to home.

Her early novels reinforced that southern connection: *Delta Wedding* in 1946 and *The Ponder Heart* in 1954 (along with her 1949 story collection, *The Golden Apples*, which deserves to be studied as a linked fiction). It is one of the ironies of writers' reputations in the States that critics prefer novels to short stories, and they accordingly judge a writer's skill on the basis of longer works. For the modernist writer Sherwood Anderson, for example, whose stories in *Winesburg, Ohio* and later collections changed the craft of short narrative, such a tendency was deadly: Anderson's novels were never as good as his shorter fictions. In Welty's case, too, more critical attention has been paid to her novels rather than to her many, many short stories that are simply superlative. It is this critical fixation on the novel that has kept Welty from winning the only prize that remains for her to achieve, the Nobel in Literature.

Welty won the Pulitzer Prize for Fiction in 1973—for a novel, *The Optimist's Daughter*, which followed her 1970 novel, *Losing Battles*. Besides O. Henry Prizes, Guggenheim fellowships, and many other awards, she has won the American Book Award, the National Endowment for the Arts' National Medal of Arts, the National Book

Foundation Medal, the National Institute of Arts and Letters Gold Medal, the President's Medal of Freedom, and the Commonwealth Award of the Modern Language Association. She has also been awarded France's Chevalier de l'Ordre des Arts et Lettres, a prize which confers knighthood.

In some ways, Welty's great skill—and the appropriate recognition that has accompanied her publications—has blunted critical need to discover new women writers. But in 1944 there was also Lillian Smith, a white writer whose good novel *Strange Fruit* brought the attention of the literary world to the continuing crimes against blacks in the South. There was Josefina Niggli, a professor in North Carolina, whose 1945 novel *Mexican Village* was followed in 1947 with *Step Down, Elder Brother,* a novel that showed the interest in her narratives of Mexican-American life when it was chosen a Book of the Month Club selection. And there has been Elizabeth Spencer, whose friendship with Welty led to her being relegated to that blanket category of "southern" woman writer even if her work, and her life, has hardly supported such a designation.

Spencer's 1948 *Fire in the Morning* was followed by her most clearly "southern" fiction, *This Crooked Way* (1952) and *The Voice at the Back Door* (1956). But with her 1960 *The Light in the Piazza,* published first in *The New Yorker* and then filmed by MGM, Spencer achieved the kind of international authority as novelist that her work deserved. Living first in Italy and then in Montreal, the Mississippian Spencer wrote her careful and never predictable novels and stories with consistent effort and polished effect.

Spencer's early career coincided with the publications of two other truly seminal women writers, Jean Stafford and Shirley Jackson. Stafford's *Boston Adventure,* 1944, was reviewed as a good realistic narrative about the immigrant poor in Chichester, near the great city. "Because we were very poor and could not buy another bed," the novel begins, "I used to sleep on a pallet made of old coats and comforters in the same room with my mother and father."[15] Stafford's "I" is Sonie Marburg, young daughter of a Russian émigré and her German shoemaker husband. The imaginary life of the sensitive child revolves around the proper and somewhat grim Miss Pride, who stays summers at the Hotel Barstow (where both mother and daughter work) and then returns to Boston to live for the year. The existence Sonie dreams of with this respectable woman contrasts with her life of hunger and humiliation resulting from her parents' drinking and fighting; finally, Hermann, guilty over being a lapsed Catholic and a failure, abandons his pregnant wife and Sonie.

The tough narrative moves between the crazy behavior of Sonie's mother and the child's attempts to keep the household solvent and stable—it is never a pleasant story. But Sonie endures and does come to live with Miss Pride and the same characters who had populated the Hotel Barstow so many years earlier. More than just Sonie's story, *Boston Adventure* is a moving description of class difference and stifled opportunities early in the twentieth century.

Critics responded even more warmly to Stafford's *The Mountain Lion* in 1947. A symbolic but also realistic tale of sibling rivalry between Molly and Ralph, the novella draws readers in through its quiet simplicity; but it ends with a storm of repressed feeling, even hatred. The lion lies dying, small and feminine: "'She's so little,' said Ralph softly. . . . 'Why, she isn't any bigger than a dog. She isn't as *big*.'"[16] The long hours and days of the men's hunting, as Ralph and Uncle Claude compliment each other on their shots even as they realize that no one can tell whose bullet had done the killing, become subsumed into the greater tragedy of the death of Molly, another small, fragile, female body. The narrative has been frequently described as "Jamesian": the ways Stafford achieves her effects continued to be remarkable.

The New Yorker then began soliciting short stories from the young California writer (who had been already married to and divorced from poet Robert Lowell). Her work appeared there in the company of stories by both Elizabeth Spencer and Shirley Jackson, particularly Jackson's rivetingly mysterious "The Lottery" in 1949. The 1950s became the decade of Jackson. Her output ranged from comic yet wry accounts of being mother to a household of children (*Life Among the Savages*, 1953, and *Raising Demons*, 1957), reminiscent of the writing of Jean Kerr, to ghostly and suggestive tales that showed her understanding of Freudian psychology (*Hangsaman*, 1951; *The Haunting of Hill House*, 1959). Like Stafford, Jackson marshaled her wit in countless narratives that treated themes of particular interest to women; she also wrote feminist stories like *The Bird's Nest* (1954). Just a few years before her early death in 1965, she published *We Have Always Lived in the Castle* (1962). There, the author's feminist consciousness meets the supernatural, and the sisters who have been socially isolated as survivors of a murder are transposed into modern witches.

Paralleling Jackson's prolific publications were those of Flannery O'Connor, whose first story collection appeared in 1955. *A Good Man Is Hard to Find and Other Stories* followed her first novel, *Wise Blood* (1952), and continued the meteoric rise of her reputation. Had readers been given the opportunity to link Shirley Jackson with Flannery O'Connor, they would have recognized a mutual interest in unexpectedly humorous (and scathingly droll) social commentary. As it was, the two writers were separated—Jackson, the wife of noted literary critic Stanley Edgar Hyman, closeted in the Bennington faculty wife category; O'Connor relegated to that larger group of southern gothic writers. O'Connor's other books are *The Violent Bear It Away* (1960) and a posthumously published second collection of stories, *Everything That Rises Must Converge* (1965).

In this brief glance at important American women fiction writers at midcentury, it is interesting to note that most of them—at one time or another—were considered popular writers rather than serious ones. Shirley Jackson in particular was a commercial success, as was Jean Stafford. The conundrum of assessing the quality and lasting merit of writers who make money has never been solved, but there does appear to be a gender difference. Ernest Hemingway and F. Scott Fitzgerald had no difficulty being profitable and serious simultaneously; Norman Mailer's books appear on best-seller lists and get reviewed by the most established critics.

We have previously viewed the 1950s as a conservative decade, even a repressed one, dominated by the suspicion and fear of the McCarthy hearings and coercing its young to grow up responsible, God fearing, and well educated. The pervasive worry of the 1950s was that one might be different, as novels and sociological studies with titles like *The Man in the Grey Flannel Suit, The Organization Man,* and *The Lonely Crowd* document. The conservative face remained tightly in place, or so it seemed, through much of the decade: only certain kinds of readers—adventurous, radical—read Allen Ginsberg's "Howl" or Jack Kerouac's *On the Road;* and the market for Henry Miller's *Tropics* remained underground.

By the end of the period, however, events like the riotous mocking of the House Un-American Activities Committee at a San Francisco hearing in 1959 (celebrated in the film *Operation Abolition*), movies like *Dr. Strangelove* (1964), and, of course, the burgeoning Civil Rights movement, made it clear that under that conformist lid extraordinarily diverse cultural energies were simmering. The

1950s, as John Updike points out, were never so simple as random memories suggest: not without ambition and information, the maligned "decade was trying to reinvent pleasure and irony."[17] Its writers had been nourished by the overwhelmingly important modernism that had fostered William Faulkner, Ernest Hemingway, Gertrude Stein, T. S. Eliot, John Steinbeck, William Carlos Williams, and other giants. What they found to create during and after the 1950s reflected currents of energy that were both forward looking and nostalgic.

6

The Quest for America

Because so much writing by women was marketed as popular fiction and because so much reading by women was denigrated as "entertainment" reading, most observers of the literary scene were interested largely, and sometimes exclusively, in fiction by men. There were a number of overlapping qualities and themes, if one compared the popular and women's novel at midcentury with what was categorized as serious, contemporary (and eventually postmodern) writing. Most writers in the 1950s were concerned with what the end of the brutalizing war meant for human goodness, what the return of men from military action meant to ongoing sexual relationships, what a world without war meant for children. Most writers continued to use modernist techniques and tried to find organic forms that would reflect their fiction's themes—innovation was still valuable, though stable narrative structures with beginnings, middles, and endings were never out of fashion.

The worlds of popular and serious reading grew increasingly separate, however. If one read the fiction of John Barth, Kurt Vonnegut Jr., William Styron, or Donald Barthelme, he or she probably turned up a sophisticated nose at Edna Ferber, Frances Parkinson Keyes, or even Shirley Jackson and Jean Stafford.

Judging from literary criticism of the 1950s and the 1960s, critics found the mode of midcentury expressed at its most vivid in the short stories and novels of J. D. Salinger. Read first in *The New Yorker*, many of his fictions opened new avenues for assessing what a story was—what the intent, the purpose, of fiction was to be. As Ihab H. Hassan points out in *Radical Innocence*, most postwar readers still believed in the role of the novel "to organize experience and to mediate between various levels of perception in culture."[1] "Art" was of some efficacy and continued to serve a moral function.

When Salinger's *The Catcher in the Rye* was a Book of the Month Club selection in 1951, its appearance shook the reading world. Retrospectively, Hassan uses the term *apotheosis* to describe the effect Salinger's work had on readers, and he couples Salinger with Dostoyevsky: his point is that Salinger had created "the new look of the American Dream, specifically dramatized by the encounter between a vision of innocence and the reality of guilt."[2] Salinger's *Catcher* extended the opposition between the 1940s stories of childhood and adolescence (as written by McCullers, Stafford, Spencer, and Capote) and those "war novels" that had been criticized for being exploitative, overly sexual, and—perhaps necessarily—inhumane. Salinger's placing Holden Caulfield's naïveté against his friends' callous use of people illustrates disparate human behavior. It is Holden who could not "make" it in the competitive world: he failed four of his five subjects. Yet even during his last weekend on campus his schoolmates want him to write their essays for them.

Hassan calls *The Catcher in the Rye* America's "testament of loss."[3] Because Holden will not accept the phoniness and mendacity of his culture, he is declared insane, unfit to live in the real world. Yet what Caulfield longs to do, as he tells his worried sister, Phoebe, is save "all these kids playing some game in this big field of rye and all. Thousands of little kids, and nobody's around—nobody big, I mean—except me. And I'm standing at the end of some crazy cliff.... I'd just be the catcher in the rye and all."[4] The stigma of Holden's caring makes him a misfit, but his contempt for other adolescent boys who are similarly out of place in their culture—Ackley, James Castle—makes him less saint than sinner. Accordingly, he knows guilt. He does not like the bothersome Ackley; he had not wanted to lend James Castle his sweater. Confronted with the kindly nuns, Holden blows smoke in their faces. Confronted with the young prostitute, "Sunny," Holden wants neither to hold her nor to pay her. The choices life presents to him seem wrong, particularly the choices Mr. Antolini offers during his overnight visit.

Like Holden, the reader needs to escape. Salinger's protagonist writes in his familiar blend of candor and disguise, "I walked all the way back to the hotel. Forty-one gorgeous blocks. I didn't do it because I felt like walking or anything. It was more because I didn't feel like getting in and out of another taxicab."[5] Holden's choices result from his being defeated, and the culture that surrounds him does, indeed, seem daunting—materialistic, greedy, supercilious, bored and boring, and usually unkind.

Salinger's "answer" to the comfortable notion that postwar culture was "normal"—that anyone who survived the outright battle of World War II should be able to resume conventional life—is one huge interrogation. What is wrong with Holden Caulfield, the voice of ennui and despair (at age sixteen)? What is wrong with Holden's family, tellingly absent from most of the narrative (his favorite brother a suicide, another brother living across country and unable to come home for the holidays, parents that are well meaning but angry)? Moving beyond Salinger's intimate characterizations, we might ask what was wrong with the American family, the basis for that famed American dream?

In the decade of Erik Erikson's *Childhood and Society* (1950), buffeted by R. D. Laing's contention that personal insanity might be an alternative response to the mad contemporary world, sophisticated readers were resistant to the conventional image of the heterosexual—and nuclear—family. The nuclear family was the way of modern life. Moving thousands of miles away from extended family bases and the known quantity of community, breadwinners in search of big money took their young families into strange territory. A 12th-floor New York apartment is hardly "home" for Holden. Salinger's protagonist searches for some adult who will act compassionately toward him: even his 10-year-old sister, Phoebe, knows that his own father "will kill him."[6]

Holden Caulfield, complete with his winningly vulgar language, becomes the bad boy of twentieth-century American letters, modernizing Twain's Huck Finn in terms of income level, lifestyle, and sexual adventurousness. But what Salinger's novel shows so clearly is that Holden is missing the kernel of spirit that makes Huck successful. Huck Finn knows whom to listen to, whom to trust. That his mentor is often Jim, the runaway slave, is a great tribute to Huck's perspicacity. The almost frantic narrative of *The Catcher in the Rye* tries to replicate a boy's successful quest, but in every case, Holden's search disappoints him. Salinger's censure falls less on his modern American boy than it does on that boy's society.

For writer Kay Boyle, Salinger's novel—like books by McCullers, James Jones, and Capote—is "essentially tragic . . . heartbreaking in the stories of loneliness they tell but tragically illuminating, too, because the protagonists in them are Americans who strive not to be considered outcasts on their own soil."[7] For the long-expatriated Boyle, able to observe American behavior and American fiction from a slightly distanced perspective, the new isolation of not only the individual but the family had created a new theme in contemporary writing. Boyle asks, however, knowing that writers have usually been outside the social mainstream, why this 1950s emphasis on "brotherly communion," on men "longing to be identified with other men."[8] Surely, she notes, the artist knows "from the beginning that he does not belong."[9]

The writer may know the condition of either existential or writerly separation, but the phenomenon attacking 1950s American fiction was more pervasive than a single strand of subject matter. Hassan, too, finds a number of novels illustrative of "the sad reality of human failure."[10] What had changed in the fiction of postwar America was that the failed person was not different from the successful person; all criteria seemed buried in one deep subjective morass, and for the rational, intelligent reader the lack of even a labyrinthine thread of meaning was frightening. The sudden if not inexplicable suicide of Seymour Glass in Salinger's story "A Perfect Day for Bananafish" plays on the same set of reader sensibilities. Seymour is habitually kind to the child Sybil; with her, he creates the kind of innocent world that he can bear. With his wife, who is mesmerized by postwar material success, he can find nothing in common. In Salinger's presentation, no one is "wrong" and no one, unfortunately, is right. Response to his fiction when it appeared in *The New Yorker* showed how unnerving readers found it.

Fictions of Disguise

Few writers wanted to face the anguish of a culture that could not find its direction, no matter how prosperous it appeared. For British critic Bernard Bergonzi, who finds *The Catcher in the Rye* "a novel of even greater intricacy than *Invisible Man*,"[11] American writers in the 1950s faced a rare imaginative dilemma: "The difficulty is, of course, that American reality is constantly transcending itself, moving to new heights of absurdity or horror that leave the most extravagantly inventive novelist behind."[12] Salinger wrote one kind of response to the times—that of withdrawal combined with quest—but many other novelists attempted to find expression through indirection. The mid-fifties became the age of erudite academic tapestries. William Gaddis's monumental *The Recognitions* (1955) asks readers to pull a number of specialized fields, particularly those of music and art, into their ken in order to literally figure out his novel. Whether or not Wyatt Gwyon would become a household name,

The Recognitions is an emphatic statement that fiction existed to create different worlds.

The fifties were also the information age, a kind of technological apex for writers—and readers—who had long been fascinated by science fiction, science fantasy, utopias and dystopias. Somewhat ironically, in this age of competition with that other world power, the Soviet Union, Vladimir Nabokov, a Russian who since 1940 had been a United States citizen, thought he had found a means of intriguing readers by writing so intricately that language and structure themselves became primary. American readers found Nabokov first through translations of his Russian novels, but by 1955 he was acclaimed for the fanciful *Lolita*, a work that might have been repellent if read for content alone. The kind of energy that marks his 1957 novel, *Pnin*, his 1962 novel, *Pale Fire* (in which he challenges all narrative conventions of character), and his 1969 novel, *Ada* (a palimpsest of his earlier fictions, filled with mentions of both *Lolita* and *Pale Fire*) was and continues to be an influence on other writers. Thomas Pynchon, for one, became famous for his elaborate *V* in 1963, followed by the more comedic *The Crying of Lot 49* in 1966. In all these texts, the reader's role is one of applauding the conventions—or the disruptions from the conventions—of writing itself.

Both Nabokov and Pynchon, joined in 1965 by Jerzy Kosinski (*The Painted Bird, Steps, Being There*), became exemplars of the new writer—one who was less isolated in a traditional ivory tower and within traditional fields of humanistic knowledge, having mastered at least the vestiges of physics, computer science, and other technologically based ways of learning and living that were beginning to dominate American consciousness.

Yet as Frederick R. Karl points out, the very intricacy that attracted some readers drove others away. Nabokov's limitation as a writer is that his creation of word and play, "reality and reflection as the sole place worthy of his inhabitancy,"[13] mandates the reader's expert interpretation of his act of writing. Nabokov, too, creates a literature of "exhaustion and enervation . . . behind the inventiveness, the glossy surfaces, the reverberating wit and witticisms, the brilliant combinations of language and languages, the introduction of Russian and French as supplemental voices, the rarefied sensibility working on every page, the parodic sense seeping into crevices and seams, the seamlessness itself of the various levels of narrative."[14]

This fiction, so often described as brilliant, might not repay some readers' effort.

The inherent separation between what a work of fiction "means" and what its convolutions of language and form might suggest to its reader came under scrutiny as literary and art critics began to be dissatisfied with formulaic analysis. Certain kinds of fiction were predictable—and, therefore, of less than consuming interest: Ernest Hemingway's 1952 *The Old Man and the Sea,* beloved for its parable-like insistence on the human values of endurance and pride, had nothing technically new to show the aspiring writer. John Cheever's short stories, like his Wapshot novels, were fairly traditional descriptions of manners, of characters easily identified by their occupations and their marriages (or their divorces). As Andreas Huyssen speculates, the rage for modernism and its techniques had leveled off, and by the 1960s "artists and critics alike shared a sense of a fundamentally new situation. The assumed postmodern rupture with the past was felt as a loss: art and literature's claims to truth and human value seemed exhausted, the belief in the constitutive power of the modern imagination just another delusion."[15]

In this view, nothing from the past has value, and very little has artistic credibility. Insisting somewhat contradictorily that education and sheer learning had maintained their worth, novelists drew from other fields of art, of science, of technology, bringing into play the idea of "the global village of McLuhanacy, the new Eden of polymorphous perversity, Paradise Now, as the Living Theater proclaimed it on stage."[16] Set as it was in the midst of the media-hyped postwar complacency, this turn away from the known to what was often the avant-garde, the European, the shocking, or the simply impenetrable was an attempt to break through the facade of uniformity that suburbia, prefabricated homes, and supermarkets suggested. Beneath the crust of the conventional, a number of different eruptions were building.

One of the most eruptive authors of the postwar period was John Barth. Apparently a scholar, Barth knew the traditional novelistic forms well—yet when he seemed to replicate them, he created parodies (or, in some cases, travesties). As Leslie A. Fiedler, one of his earliest champions, notes, Barth works up the past not to find truth but rather to chart absurdity. His is history "irreverently interpreted."[17] In the case of *The Sot-Weed Factor,* Barth's antihistorical

historical novel of Ebenezer Cooke, poet laureate of Maryland, the book is "a joke book, an endless series of gags."[18]

Fiedler assesses the themes of the novel as being dominated by subjects objectionable to readers in 1960—brother-sister incest, comradeship among men that comes "perilously close to"[19] homosexuality, and antiheroic behavior under the guise of innocence and evasion of responsibility. Descriptions of sex are no longer disguised: one of the funniest of the segments is a madcap misidentification of Susan Warren, who is alternately a wife, whore, opium addict, swineherd, pig, and doppelgänger of Ebenezer's Joan Toast. The son of her master, Mitchell, himself mistaken for a woman in the pigsty, reveals to Eben that his true love is a pig:

"Thou'rt in love with Susan?" Ebenezer asked incredulously.

"Aye and I am," Tim Mitchell replied, "and have been since the day I saw her. Her name is really Portia, Mister Cooke; 'tis Father calls her Susie, after a whore of a mistress he once had. He regards her as his property, sir, and treats her like a beast! Should he learn the truth of our love there would be no end to his wrath!"

Ebenezer's brain spun dizzily. "Dear Mister Mitchell-"

"The blackguard!" Timothy went on, his voice unsteady. "Till he hath got that new wench in his power, he comes out eveningly to poor sweet Portia, whose maidenhead he claimed when she was yet a shoat too young to fend him off."

Ebenezer could not but admire the metaphor of the shoat, and yet there were obvious discrepancies between the accounts of Susan's past. "I do declare," he protested, "this is not—"

"There is no limit to the man's poltroonery," Timothy hissed. "Albeit he is my father, sir, I loathe him like the Devil. Say naught of this, I beg ye, for in his wickedness, did he know aught of our love, he would give her to the lecherous boar in yonder pen, that e'er hath looked on her with lewd intent, and let him take his slavering will o' her."

Ebenezer gasped. "You do not mean to say—"

But even as the truth dawned on him, young Mitchell called "Portia! Hither, Portia! Soo-ie!" and an animal shuffled over from the far wall in the dark.[20]

The lusty fantasy of Eben Cooke's odyssey is overlaid with the irony of his own carefully preserved chastity. In this role reversal, Barth rewrites the countless narratives of virginal women, always signaling his readers that comedy is his main intent. Language which recalls that of the traditional historical novel is set against the double entendre, the pun, and—as in this quotation—the misleading use of *metaphor* to create unexpected dramatic irony. Replete with narratives that cross and intersect, with misadventures and mistold stories, *The Sot-Weed Factor* is a compendium of rich language. Much of its comedy is epistemological.

For the aging poet protagonist Ebenezer, however, the loss of his virginity parallels the loss of his artistic power. Even as his writing brings him increasing fame, he realizes how slight his art has been: "*The Sot-Weed Factor* itself he came to see as an artless work, full of clumsy spleen, obscure allusions, and ponderous or merely foppish levities; and none of his later conceptions struck him as worthy of the pen."[21] No longer poet laureate, Cooke earns his living through various clerical duties. But the novel ends happily, once Eben returns to his writing and completes a sequel to his famous book before he dies. With Barth's satisfied flourish, Cooke writes his own overblown if satiric epitaph, and the fiction ends, all narratives concluded, all characters answered for, and the moral system reestablished in the writer's universe. By returning to the formal narrative shape of a more orderly past world, Barth enables his fiction to itself create stability for the reader. Escaping the world of postwar horror for the more limited, and recognizable, adventures of an eighteenth-century picaro gives the reader, at the very least, a period of repose.

Barth's early fiction is thoroughly self-conscious, and it has accordingly become representative of what critics were to later call postmodern, self-reflexive narrative. Like Gaddis, Barth draws to some extent on musical references and forms (his first two novels, *The Floating Opera* in 1956 and *The End of the Road* in 1958, are often discussed as being jazzlike improvisations—Barth was a music student early in his career). More visibly, however, both those works are parodic—*Opera* responding to Camus's existential angst by showing that suicide may not be positive, *Road* reflecting the immense and sometimes wearying influence in intellectual circles of Jean-Paul Sartre. In a similar vein, *The Sot-Weed Factor* drew from Barth's enthusiasm for the unworldly, parabolic works of Jorge Luis Borges, answering in kind Borges's short fiction "Pierre Menard, Author of Don Quixote." In 1966, his *Giles Goat-Boy, or The Revised New Syllabus* attempted science fantasy, or at least utopian fiction; in 1968, the fictional experiments collected in *Lost in the Funhouse*, particularly its title narrative, proved Barth's great inventiveness. Unlike some postwar novelists, however, this author shows through both his own innovative production and his criticism of contemporary fiction that he was helping to shape cultural change.

Barth's 1967 *Atlantic Monthly* essay, "The Literature of Exhaustion," gave the literary world a trope which dominated discussion for the next decade. The author was careful to point out that he used the term to describe not any outworn "physical, moral, or intellectual decadence" but rather "the used-upness of certain forms or exhaustion of certain possibilities—by no means necessarily a cause for despair."[22] In his own novels, Barth was showing how that very "used-upness" could work in the writer's favor, because familiarity with those forms meant readers could readily understand his parodic reinscriptions. Without knowing what an eighteenth-century historical novel is like, someone reading *The Sot-Weed Factor* would have less fun. Barth's primary point in this brief essay, however, is that "art and its forms and techniques live in history and certainly do change."[23] While being technically up to date may not be the most important consideration in judging contemporary fiction, for Barth the *sensibility* of the contemporary must be present in truly fine writing:

A good many current novelists write turn-of-the-century-type novels, only in more or less mid-twentieth-century language and about contemporary people and topics; this makes them considerably less interesting (to me) than excellent writers who are also technically contemporary: Joyce and Kafka, for instance, in their time, and in ours, Samuel Beckett and Jorge Luis Borges.[24]

Influential as his own fiction has been, Barth's opinion here also carries weight and continues to build appreciation for the wry, parodic, multilayered novel.

The Fiction of Parody

Because the modernists had some success in promoting their vision of civilization as a disappointing, frightening phenomenon, a tone of despair kept the literature of much of this century serious: what humor did exist was created through irony. Angst at the ultimate recognition—the meaninglessness of life—underlies some of the best-known literature written from the time of World War I through the depressed 1930s and into World War II. After the atomic bomb was used in that war, a great many writers chose the humor of ironic understatement as a basis for their philosophy. If all life is hopeless, if rational order has given way to the random and the accidental, then forbearance is one of a human being's most essential traits. Endurance can count for something.

During the 1930s Nathanael West's fiction—and more than a little of Faulkner's—had prepared the way for incongruous but convincing views of the contemporary scene in such 1950s books as Salinger's *The Catcher in the Rye,* Saul Bellow's *The Adventures of Augie March,* Shirley Jackson's *Hangsaman,* John Hawkes's *The Beetle Leg,* Randall Jarrell's *Pictures from an Institution,* Kurt Vonnegut Jr.'s *Player Piano,* and Flannery O'Connor's *Wise Blood.* O'Connor's macabre world surely speaks of radical changes in attitudes among American readers. Only because she was a southerner was O'Connor not considered a sensationalist or worse: she must be writing about what she knows, critics decided, thereby also deciding that O'Connor's South must be a strange world. Yet as O'Connor continued writing her fiction throughout the 1950s and into the 1960s, she insisted that the truths of her narratives were more than southern. Hers was an art of observation, of withdrawal, and yet—simultaneously—of compassion. The distance of the ideal modernist had been replaced with a new use of humor, the writer laughing not at despicable characters but at the world which produced them—and never with real laughter but with a breath-held and usually hidden grin of recognition. This combination of existentialist and southern humor and a powerful mysticism gives O'Connor's fiction its staying power.

One of the most important of America's postwar parodists, John Hawkes, praises O'Connor—along with Nathanael West and Djuna Barnes—for being "together in that rare climate of pure and immoral *creation,*" although he sees that they form an exclusive company. According to Hawkes, the three writers "are very nearly alone in their uses of wit, their comic treatments of violence and their extreme detachment."[25] He then fits these admirable qualities into a larger definition of the contemporary novel:

> If the true purpose of the novel is to assume a significant shape and to objectify the terrifying similarity between the unconscious desires of the solitary man and the disruptive needs of the volatile world, then the satiric writer, running maliciously at the head of the mob and creating the shape of his meaningful psychic paradox as he goes, will serve best the novel's purpose.[26]

Fellow novelist Saul Bellow echoes Hawkes's proclivities: "The private and inner life which was the subject of serious books until very recently now begins to have an antique and funny look. The earnestness of a Proust toward himself would seem old-fashioned today."[27] Championing humor of a certain kind—that having to do with "the disintegrating outline of the worthy and humane Self, the bourgeois hero of an earlier age"[28]—Bellow praises the work of J. P. Donleavy (*The Ginger Man*), Nabokov (*Lolita*), and Bruce J. Friedman's *Stern*. He concludes that much contemporary fiction is not yet dealing with the pressing issues of anomie, self-discovery, and self-disgust: recent books, rather, "have told us, indignantly or nihilistically or comically, how great our error is, but for the rest they have offered us thin fare."[29]

Both Hawkes's *Second Skin* and Bellow's *Henderson the Rain King* play on those facets of comedy—or, in Hawkes's case, the macabre—described in their essays. Ironizing the human situations of their male protagonists, each novelist creates a narrative that shows how fragile human life is, how inadequate human reason is to ferret out the motivation of others. Skipper, Hawkes's enduring but hardly heroic character, tells a crowded and unsteady story. He supposedly describes his own life, that of what he calls his "harmless and sanguine self."[30] In reality, however, *Second Skin* is a mystically nightmarish account of a man who thinks he can control the people he loves; what happens in Skipper's life proves that men seldom have such control.

Ihab H. Hassan calls Hawkes's work both "gothic" and "surrealistic";[31] he also links his vision with that of Nathanael West. As placeless as it is formless, Hawkes's fiction merges land with water, heterosexuality with homosexuality, elitism with banality, and pleasure with pain in a blurred narrative that seems to be achronological. Whether it be the British racing underworld of *The Lime Twig* or the New England seacoast of *Second Skin*, location in Hawkes's work is as irrelevant as time. The dreamlike effects of Skipper's narration—absent fact, description, and even event—disorient the reader so that nothing comes as a surprise. The most brutal scenes move back into the atmosphere of calm—yet that calm is drenched with the results of horrors seldom included in fiction of the early 1960s.

At the center of *Second Skin* is one of the author's compelling juxtapositions of event. First Skipper, trying to be helpful to his daughter, Cassandra, finds his missing son-in-law Fernandez—or his badly mutilated body. In a memory that appears and reappears throughout the text, Skipper comes to the room on Second Avenue, faces the bloody nakedness of his son-in-law, and faces as well the fact that this "little fairy spic"[32] who is his daughter's husband is also the lover of sailors on leave. In the bloody room, Fernandez (and one of the sailors who tries to defend him) has been killed for sport by homophobic men.

Inconceivable to Skipper, who is an aging but still idealistic rebel-victim, such murder leaves him stunned—and he does not tell Cassandra of her husband's death for several months. His introspection about his decision later haunts him, and he recalls:

[I]. . . *dropped to my knees beside her and took her cold hand—no rings—and confessed to her at long last that Fernandez was dead. That I had found him dead at the end of my final shore patrol on Second Avenue. That I thought she should know.*

Yes, I thought she should know. And yes, I told her the truth, made my confession, got it off my chest that night the snow fell into the trembling arms of the larch trees on our black and ragged island rooted fast in the cold and choppy waters of the Atlantic. Yes, I told her, my own daughter. For her own good. For her own good and mine, for our mutual relief. And yes, yes, I thought she might spare herself if she knew the truth, might spare her own life somehow. But I was wrong, of course.

The truth. Yet wasn't I deceiving her even then? Wasn't I sparing her certain details, withholding others, failing somehow to convey the true tonality of the thing? Well, I should hope to God![33]

Philosophy, humanism, truth, the right behavior—Skipper questions the anticipated correct responses in his sad inquiry. Then, immediately, Skipper moves from his grief as father to his grief as son, in the poignant scene that shows him as Edward, the pudgy child, trying to prevent his father's suicide.

"Papa," I cried, "no, Papa. Please. . . ."
"I shall do it, Edward, I tell you. See if I don't. . . ."
"But please, please, what about Mamma, Papa? What about me?"
"Some things, Edward, can't be helped. . . ."
And crouching at the keyhold of the lavatory door, soft little hands cupped on soft fat knees and hot, desperate, hopeful, suddenly inspired: "Wait, Papa, wait, I will play for you, poor Papa."
"No, no, Edward, never mind . . . it will do no good. . . ."[34]

Rushing to get his cello to play the Brahms, the "small and fat and ungainly" child tried to put off the inevitable tragedy: "I ran to my room though I was not a quick child, ran with my short plump bare arms flung out in front of me and not a sob in my throat, not a snuffle in my little pink naked rosebud of a nose, so bent was I on staying his hand with my cello."[35] But his father put a bullet through his head nevertheless.

Hawkes's accomplished and textured poetic prose keeps any sense of reality suspended, except when (as in this moving scene) he brings the conventions of realism into play. All at once, the shadowy Skipper, a man fraught with problems in his relationships, comes alive in that desperate little boy, a boy whose frustration at his inability to save his father anticipates Skipper's later frustration when he tries to do what is best for his own child. In each case he fails.

Although Saul Bellow's Henderson is cut from the same cloth— both Skipper and he are well-intentioned white men, forcing themselves to play their powerful roles in the patriarchy—in the author's choice of an absurdist plot, he gives new focus to the dilemma of aging men. *Henderson the Rain King* is comic largely because of its remove to Africa—but the problems of impotence of various kinds track the protagonist even to remote locations. Within the apparent disjunctions of Bellow's 1959 novel are scenes that clearly echo the failures of Joseph in *Dangling Man, The Victim, Augie March,* and Tommy Wilhelm in *Seize the Day*—and predict the emotional tone of *Herzog.*

Never just a picaresque adventure, *Henderson* is built around those confrontational dialogues that advertise Bellow's concern with philosophy. In the midst of the (admittedly comic) frog killing, for example, Henderson chastises the loyal Romilayu:

"Now, you've got to quit this, Romilayu. I am entitled to your trust, this once. I tell you it is going to work."

"Yes, sah," he said.

"I don't want you to think I'm not capable of doing a good job."

He said again, "Yes, sah."

"There is that poem about the nightingale singing that humankind cannot stand too much reality. But how much unreality can it stand? Do you follow? You understand me?"

"Me unnastand, sah."

"I fired that question right back at the nightingale. So what if reality may be terrible? It's better than what we've got."

"Kay, sah. Okay."

"All right, I let you out of it. It's better than what I've got. But every man feels from his soul that he has got to carry his life to a certain depth. Well, I have to go on because I haven't reached that depth yet. You get it?"

"Yes, sah."

"Hah! Life may think it has got me written off in its records. Henderson: type so and so, with the auk and the platypus and other experiments illustrating such-and-such a principle, and laid aside. But life may find itself surprised, for after all, we are men. I am Man—I myself, singular as it may look. Man. And man has many times tricked life when life thought it had him trapped."[36]

This scene has all the trappings of a serious (and quotable) central point in the novel: "meaning," self-scrutiny (for the literal inability of the two men to communicate because of their language difference emphasizes how isolated Henderson is), Henderson's own resolution. Taking his explosive charge in his hands, the wealthy American WASP is about to show the world—and the universe—of what he is made. Not a likely showcase, this tiny African village will applaud. (Literarily, it all works for Conrad in *The Heart of Darkness*.) Henderson's failure as he destroys not only the frogs but the water supply itself is a despairing answer to his incipient dialogue with a larger life force.

Later, captured by the less amicable tribe of Wariri, Henderson imagines his answering their questions ("What was the purpose of my trip, and why was I traveling like this?") in the same solipsistic language. By this time, he has learned what he cannot say:

Nor: "You see, Mr. Examiner, everything has become so tremendous and involved, why, we're nothing but instruments of this world's processes."

Nor: "I am this kind of guy, rest is painful to me, and I have to have motion."

Nor: "I'm trying to learn something, before it all gets away from me."

As you can see for yourselves, these are all impossible answers. . . .[37]

Reviewed as a comic masterpiece, *Henderson the Rain King* may have been an important influence on Hawkes's *Second Skin*. Here too, Henderson laments what has become of his son, playing his life away in California, that mecca for the unconventional, and tries to save him from the lures of pure pleasure: "a father is a father after all, and I had gone as far as California to try to talk to Edward."[38]

Here, Bellow relies on the epistemology of generational, and cultural, difference. When Henderson tries out his brand of language, claiming to be a fighter—"for the truth. Yes, that's it, the truth. Against falsehood"—Edward, of course, knows him too well to pretend to listen. Another failed mission for Henderson. In his self-protective reflection, however, he blames their lack of connection on his son: "I understood very well that Edward wanted me to tell him what he should live for and this is what was wrong. This was what caused me pain. For every son expects and every father wishes to provide clear principles. And moreover a man wants to protect his children from the bitterness of things if he can."[39] Henderson does not commit suicide within sight of his son, as Hawkes's father does, but he has provided almost none of the guidance that children might have reason to expect.

Bruce Bawer notes in a recent study that *Henderson* "is the exuberant yet strangely solemn story of an adventurer, a man in search of self-definition who at novel's end claims to have learned a thing or two about life but who has not really changed at all."[40] The fact that one of the most "comic" novels of the 1950s is seldom funny, particularly from the perspective of the end of the century, sheds crucial light on why critics may have been eager to classify work at midcentury as ironic, parodic, or comic. Immersed as they were in the bleak wash of existential search, surrounded in all languages by serious if conventional treatments of self-scrutiny, the best readers of the times were surely hungry for something other. Any relief from the intensity of postwar, postbomb, postpromise meditation would probably have been labeled—and promoted—as comedy.

This kind of subdued laughter at conformity and a restrained outrage at cold-war politics lay at the heart of many more fifties works than those by Hawkes or Bellow or O'Connor. There are the tirades—some in poetry, some in prose poems, and some in fiction—of the so-called "Beats," urban writers who chose to move West and look for acerbic humor, as well as passionate outrage, in the drop out, sexually experimental cultures there. On the other coast, in his 1959 novella *Goodbye, Columbus*, Philip Roth satirized the materialistic lives of successful suburban Jews. The positive acceptance of his writing helped to crystallize appreciation of what came to be seen as "Jewish fiction," a nomenclature that caught fire as had "southern fiction" in earlier decades. As these discussions of both *Second Skin* and *Henderson the Rain King* suggest, however, the employment of comedy and parody as a turning away from existentialist self-scrutiny during the 1950s and the early 1960s was not really such a brightening move. At base, both Skipper and Henderson remain isolated and tormented men in worlds that expect them to be powerful. Variations on their failures seem, finally, less than comic.

The turn to parody that had so excited critics and had given novelists new avenues for narrative even if not for characterization led to the creation of still another new term, that of black (or, more accurately, gallows) humor. With their fondness for permeating boundaries, writers we have elsewhere discussed—Barth, Pynchon, Donleavy, Friedman, Hawkes—along with Terry Southern, James Purdy, William S. Burroughs, and Joseph Heller are the mainstays of this category. As Burton Feldman defines it, writers in this genre share a view of life which is "audaciously 'black'—subversive, enraged, even apocalyptic."[41] It is the manner of this writing, maintaining a "coolly 'humorous,' murderously farcical, coldly zany, cosmically slapsticky"[42] tone that identifies the writers and their work.

What results from this hot-and-cold douche is an enigma. Instead of much blackness or humor, there is a nightmarish neutrality and grotesque deadpan, an elaborate novelistic impasse to feeling and judgment. But the strangest result is this: the effect of all this savage gesture and cold comedy is disappointingly mild, even harmlessly "literary."[43]

The term continued to be useful, however, as more and more writers eschewed the heavy seriousness of modernism for the more palatable pose of humor.

One of the more dramatic uses of this stance occurs in the novel of World War II, a genre, as we have seen, that is often grimly serious. In 1961, Joseph Heller's *Catch-22* won immediate acclaim for its portrayal of damaged characters caught in the vicious lunacies of military bureaucracy. Like Ken Kesey's *One Flew Over the Cuckoo's Nest*, published the following year, *Catch-22* posed questions about the absurdities of contemporary existence: to be eligible for discharge from the Air Force on grounds of insanity, for example, one could not be sane enough to apply for discharge—a typical catch-22. Randomness rules, but all interactions are absurd. Colonel Cathcart's shout to Major Major is typical: "You're the new squadron commander. . . . But don't think it means anything, because it doesn't. All it means is that you're the new squadron commander."[44]

For the complex John Yossarian, the Air Force bombardier haunted by the memory of his young friend Snowden dying, the increase in the number of missions to be flown before a man could return to the States is a death warrant. As a concrete representation of the meaningless "rules" the military creates, this increase symbolizes the moral wilderness of the patriotic establishment. Yossarian wants nothing to do with any of it, but he cannot stay in the hospital forever. And neither—given the increased number of required missions—can he legally go home.

Discussing Heller's serious, and in some ways political, humor, Eric Homberger suggests that *Catch-22* "is firmly based upon the perception (so widely to be observed in American war novels) that the old clarity between enemy and friend, them and us, was no longer meaningful in the conditions of modern warfare. . . . We see nothing of the Nazis in the novel, but 'our' side was as blandly bureaucratic, as inhumane, as uncaring, as we know 'they' were. The politics of the novel are from the Cold War, but belong more to an undercurrent of suspicion which gained ground in the 1950s that the rival states were far more akin to each other, were being reciprocally deformed by their conflict, than the proclaimed official ideologies would suggest."[45] While Heller does spend time on external political ramifications, today's reader is more often struck by the similarities between *Catch-22* and works by Bellow, Hawkes, and other nonwar novelists.

Heller, too, questions the authority of the patriarchy, complete with its anxieties of power and the many quasi father-and-son relationships. Several of his subplots are based on this theme, and it becomes explicit in the exchange between young Nately and the ancient old man. Nately asserts, "There is nothing so absurd about risking your life for your country!" But the man confronts him by reminding him, "There are now fifty or sixty countries fighting in this war. Surely so many countries can't *all* be worth dying for."[46] Heller's innocent use of Nately's vernacular leads to the next interchange:

"Anything worth living for," said Nately, "is worth dying for."

"And anything worth dying for," answered the sacrilegious old man, "is certainly worth living for. You know, you're such a pure and naive young man that I almost feel sorry for you. . . . They are going to kill you if you don't watch out, and I can see now that you are not going to watch out. Why don't you use some sense and try to be more like me? You might live to be a hundred and seven, too."

"Because it's better to die on one's feet than live on one's knees," Nately retorted with triumphant and lofty conviction. "I guess you've heard that saying before."

"Yes, I certainly have," mused the treacherous old man, smiling again. "But I'm afraid you have it backward. It is better to live on one's feet than die on one's knees. . . ."[47]

Again, epistemological conventions force the reader to interrogate why this scene occurs when it does in the novel: surely, as the old man would say, there are other ways of showing Nately's innocence. But as he repairs to a lonely sofa to spend the night, unable to find his "whore" even in the midst of the whorehouse, Nately becomes the paradigm for all those patriotic youth (he is just 19) who comprise much of the military. Trusting, believing the rhetoric, and most of all idealizing the patriotic, these adolescents are the real tragedies of war.

Nately, of course, dies. So do many of the characters Yossarian warns, and then mourns. But his own escape comes as an almost anticlimactic resolution: Frederick R. Karl notes accurately that *Catch-22* does not work like most long fictions: "The forward movement of the novel proceeds by means of brief character descriptions in which plot elements are embedded. Movement forward is slowed everywhere to allow for lateral movement, so that our sense of narrative is glacial—a large mass moving almost imperceptibly toward some resolution of the catch."[48] Concerned with all the sentient members of the military, the reader is less than reassured when Yossarian—in the midst of running away to Sweden—responds to Major Danby's question about how he feels, "Fine. No, I'm very frightened."[49]

Going AWOL is neither "living on one's knees" nor dying on them—it is more of a replication of Frederic Henry's choice in Hemingway's earlier, and simpler, war, when he and Catherine Barkley sail across the lake to say their "farewell to arms." Yossarian's choice is a literary move, not a practical military one; and it places *Catch-22*, finally, back into the literary mainstream. That, along with its tough humor, is reason enough for its longevity.

Eric Homberger concludes that by this time in twentieth-century history, World War II had become a useful and a multifaceted metaphor. Heller's work, like that of Kesey and Vonnegut, tends to "diminish the presence of the specific causes of war, and to see it as a phenomenon which is caused by man's nature: evil and fallen man's innate propensity for aggression and violence."[50]

Kurt Vonnegut Jr. chose to leave known, conventional literary patterns as his means of abandoning the establishment. Even though science fiction was hardly a reputable genre in the 1950s, he felt that its traditions suited his repertoire of critical outrage. Vonnegut may have been the most dissatisfied of the 1950s writers: humor alone would not fulfill the needs of his characters as they face contemporary American culture.

Although he was not to write his searing commentary on war until 1969, imaged in the Allies' senseless destruction of Dresden in *Slaughterhouse-five*, Vonnegut's work from *Player Piano* (1952) on cries out against the privileging of technology over people. Often, as Peter Jones notes, there is a "thematic fusion of technology (or science) and war," as if the subjects were interchangeable: *Player Piano* shows technology's "fatal influence" on a human being.[51]

Vonnegut writes in his 1959 novel, *The Sirens of Titan*, that it is "a true story for the Nightmare Ages" and that its publication falls during the time period "between the Second World War and the Third Great Depression."[52] As Vonnegut creates his own world, he points out that postwar America is the home of "a nightmare of meaninglessness without end, [a place where people are] ignorant of the truths that lie within every human being."[53] Thinking to find life's worth in technology, they forget human values. In this seriocomic narrative of ghosts who materialize every 59 days, of love denigrated to the act of breeding, and of people so pretentious as to cherish the Church of God the Utterly Indifferent, Vonnegut comments on an entire (largely upper-class, or at least moneyed) civilization. But in his 1963 novel, *Cat's Cradle*, he turns his attention to science per se, more expressly to Dr. Felix Hoenikker, one of the creators of the atomic bomb, and his real legacy to his culture—three oddly handicapped children and a substance even more destructive than the A-bomb, Ice-nine.

Literature has few characters more despicable than the revered Hoenikker. Although he has married the woman who is the town catch, he barely notices her—and at her death (when their midget son, Newt, is born) scarcely takes notice. He assumes that their oldest child, Angela, a tall, ungainly girl, will drop out of high school to become housewife and mother to her brothers. She does. The third child, Frank, is a monster of organization, and the worlds he creates—both in the toy shop where he works and in San Lorenzo, where he has a chance to become king—are his answers to the lack of love and concern in Felix Hoenikker.

What the world-famous scientist does is play games. When Hiroshima is destroyed, his day is spent at home with a piece of string. He is making a cat's cradle. When he tries to share the admittedly low-tech string creation with his lonely son Newt, the child finds the rare attention frightening and sees his father as a monster. As he recalls later for the journalist who is trying to recreate Hoenikker's life, "No wonder kids grow up crazy. A cat's cradle is nothing but a bunch of X's between somebody's hands, and little kids look and look and look at all those X's. . . . *No damn cat, and no damn cradle.*"[54]

As the characters all move to San Lorenzo, land of Bokonon, a faith established by a black economist in an O'Neillish *Emperor Jones* kind of enterprise, to be with Frank in his days of media triumph, more and more of their sad story is told. Felix *has* been a monster. Besides inventing the bomb, he has also invented Ice-nine, a substance that instantaneously changes whatever it touches to ice—and its properties are transferable because whatever the touched substance touches also becomes ice. The world as ice rather than fire is Hoenikker's real legacy. At his death (from the substance, as he smiles his way out) one Christmas Eve, his heirs divide the liquid and chips into three parts, and the childish thermos bottles they carry through life are, literally, their secret inheritance. Reminiscent of Dante's lower circles of hell in his *Inferno,* the prospect of a frozen world restricts all warmth of human interaction. Ironically, Angela uses her inheritance to buy herself a striking scientist as husband—although an unfaithful one. And Frank uses his Ice-nine to buy himself his tropical kingdom. Even Newt uses his to attract the one romance of his life.

But mere human love is hardly the issue in Vonnegut's novel. It is, rather, the end of the world as readers know it. When San Lorenzo turns inescapably to ice, the author's benediction is once more on scientific knowledge as dehumanizing influence. Critic Richard Kostelanetz refers in his introduction to *On Contemporary Literature* to the theme of "the modern world as hell," an image evoked, he says, "with a violence and intensity equally unprecedented."[55] Despite the turn to economic prosperity in America, there seemed to be surprisingly little promise in either art or life.

Postscript

Currents in Despair

If writers and readers in the 1960s were still poised on the brink of existential sadness, reacting to cultural change with the suspicion and distrust they had brought to war itself, then had there been any change at all since the depths of the 1930s Depression? Where had American fiction gone in 30 years? A more pertinent question might be, where had *America* gone in that time? Even the highly vaunted postwar prosperity had apparently done little to ameliorate the insecurities that made many Americans mistrustful of difference and threatened by moral, financial, and religious change.

As our reading of much of this fiction has indicated, World War II was the seminal experience of the mid-twentieth century. Not only its harsh catalytic force—making people accept lives (and deaths) previously inconceivable to them—but also its leavening influence on both morality and the economy meant that people who lived in the United States during the 1950s and the 1960s would be different from those who inhabited the country before the war. World War II left readers around the world weighed down with pain. Speaking of that heavy grief, Eric Homberger notes,

> There is a claim, however, which this literature taken as a whole makes on us. The war killed so many millions of people that the sheer numbers mean nothing, cannot be held in the mind no matter how easily they roll off the tongue. New terms such as "genocide" and "holocaust" have entered our vocabulary, but the reality of individual death, to say nothing of forty million dead, leaks out of western culture.... Of all the many images of war in American war novels, it is not descriptions of the dead which haunt the memory, but of transformation, the passage out of life, in which war reveals its true face.[1]

Rather than admit to such an impact, readers bought and enjoyed the increasingly comic appraisals of contemporary culture. Humor—whether it is named "black" or "gallows"—seems on the surface to have transformed the *angst* so familiar to the war years.

The ever-circumspect literary critics, behaving as they had during the Great Depression, closed their eyes to significant new currents in fiction. The wasteland of postwar American despair was at great variance with the times: how could such anguish exist during the prosperous 1950s? Surely these postwar fictions, with their almost constant metaphors of sickness if not insanity, were largely melodramatic. Except when American novelists were echoing the French existentialists, their own grim forays into guilty introspection seemed exaggerated. Books that were being commercially published tended to support this critical response: the early 1960s, in fact, for the most part, looked much like the early 1950s. Midcentury still seemed to be a complacent and prosperous era.

These appearances, however, only partially masked evidence of countless rebellions lurking off the main stage. One of those involved gender: angry women were about to find voice. In the early 1960s a new feminism began to be expressed, codified by the influential Commission on the Status of Women and by the founding of such organizations as NOW, the National Organization for Women. Betty Friedan's *The Feminine Mystique* in 1963 and Simone de Beauvoir's work gave political shape to ideas that were implicit elsewhere in the culture. Sylvia Plath's *The Bell Jar* was published in England in 1963 (under the pseudonym *Victoria Lucas*) after the two United States publishers to whom she submitted the novel had both rejected it.

The angriest woman novelist known to the critics and readers of the time was Californian Joan Didion, whose *Run River* (1963) expresses the malaise of the previously silent American female. Telling of her protagonist's violation and unexpressed anger, Didion began the important oeuvre that would include the influential *Play It as It Lays* and *A Book of Common Prayer* in the 1970s. A more comfortable woman writer, because she often writes in cadences that resemble men's voices (she's frequently compared with Faulkner), is Joyce Carol Oates. After her 1964 novel, *With Shuddering Fall*, the cascade of her memorable fiction—both short and long—began, capped in the next decade with *A Garden of Earthly Delights, Expensive People,* and the National Book Award–winning *them.* Realistic, even naturalistic, Oates eschews the label of feminist: her protagonists are men as well as women, and her male characters are as often victimized as her female.

Even as Joyce Carol Oates, a white woman writer, was describing the 1967 Detroit riots in *them,* numerous African American writers were finding both voice and publishers. Contemporary African American fiction addresses segregation and prejudice of various kinds and develops themes that fiction written for largely white audiences might have avoided for fear of offending. From early 1960, when the Greensboro, North Carolina, lunch counter sit-in led to numerous freedom rides, boycotts, and voter registration drives throughout the South, to the full expression of that nonviolent sentiment in Dr. Martin Luther King Jr.'s "I Have a Dream" speech in Washington, D.C., the necessity of accepting rightful change dawned on the country as a whole. But the struggle continued, visible particularly in the riots from 1964 on that took place in Watts, Newark, Detroit, and dozens of other black and Latino ghettos across America and immortalized by the assassinations of President John F. Kennedy and Civil Rights leader Medgar Evers in 1963, the three Mississippi freedom summer workers—Chaney, Schwerner, and Goodman—in 1964, Malcolm X in 1965, and both Robert F. Kennedy and Martin Luther King Jr. in 1968.

Interest in "minority" voices opened publishing doors to ethnic writers in general, particularly people of color. But change—even as it occurred—was difficult to acknowledge. In 1964, one influential critic divided the protagonists of serious American fiction being published in the 1960s into these categories: (1) "The hero as a child who may stand for truth or Edenic innocence, and is victimized," (2) "The lonely adolescent or youth, exposing the corrupt adult world," (3) "The lover caught in the impossible web woven by instincts and institutions around him," (4) "The Negro in search of the eternal, elusive identity which white men refuse to grant him or themselves," (5) "The Jew engaged with Gentiles," (6) "The grotesque," (7) "The underdog, most often hapless soldiers," (8) "The disinherited American," (9) "The comic picaro," (10) "The hipster." In every case except two, the novels used as illustration of these categories are by white writers; and in the other cases, the novels chosen as illustration are by men.[2] Notice that there is no category that defines important characters as those created by women; the concept of a gendered anomie did not yet exist—nor did the notion of women's writing as a category. (We have also seen that the women writers recognized by critics were described in terms other than gender: Ann Petry was considered an African American writer; Carson McCullers and Eudora Welty were southern writers; and Flannery O'Connor was a religious writer—none were named as women writers.)

With critical opinion so firmly set in recognizable—and repetitive—patterns, an outsider's breaking onto the fictional scene in any significant way was almost impossible. Literary book club choices reified what critics thought was the direction of contemporary fiction, and publishing contracts, sales, and prizes verified those choices. One bright spot on the literary horizon for the novice writer was the fact that the first half of the 1960s brought the deaths of a great number of the unquestionable leaders of twentieth-century writing: in 1960, Richard Wright and Albert Camus; in 1961, Celine, Carl Jung, H. D., Dashiell Hammett, and Ernest Hemingway (whose shocking suicide made readers question what they thought had been the import of his greatest fiction); in 1962, William Faulkner, e. e. cummings, Robinson Jeffers, and Isak Dinesen; in 1963, William Carlos Williams, Theodore Roethke, Robert Frost, Aldous Huxley, and Sylvia Plath; in 1964, Flannery O'Connor and Lorraine Hansberry; and in 1965, T. S. Eliot.

With these deaths came a kind of freedom for other writers, the concept of the anxiety of influence being more accurate than some would like to admit. To have these great writers simply gone was to remove the anticipation of what they might do next—as, for example, in the case of Faulkner, whose steady production lasted almost to the time of his death with the publication of *The Reivers* just a few weeks earlier. For the most part, however, the late work of Faulkner, Hemingway, Steinbeck (who died in 1968), and Dos Passos (whose life ended in 1970)—like that of Frost, cummings, Carl Sandburg, and Langston Hughes (both died in 1967)—has not been considered major work. There was a tone of sad nostalgia to many of the generally respectful reviews.

On the one hand, then, the great writers of the earlier twentieth century had stopped being writers of riveting interest. It is true that this attitude of blanket dismissal cost the literary world knowledge of some great writing (William Carlos Williams's later poems, for example, or Faulkner's *The Reivers,* as fine a novel as anything he had written since *Absalom, Absalom!*). But again, their virtual absence from the competitive field left the way clear for new kinds of stylistic and thematic innovation.

During the second half of the twentieth century, a period still disrupted by unacknowledged wars both abroad and at home, the primary kind of serious literary expression has been described as *postmodern*. This wry decentering of writerly, and even literary, authority helped to take readers back into the process of voicing: they learned to recognize the pained adolescent tones of John Barth's "Lost in the Funhouse" just as they chuckled aloud at the effects of Donald Barthelme's 1967 fairy tale *Snow White*. New to the concept of fiction, however, was the postmodern insistence on making the reader aware of the writing process, of the indecision and frustration and joy of the author, whether he or she appears as character or as self in the production of the text. Accepting the writer's self-conscious and self-referential pose was the first step required of readers wanting to understand metafiction. One of the philosophic bases for the postmodern is a disbelief in the primacy of known, and learned, history.

With Richard Brautigan's minimalist prose poems and poetry, works almost devoid of any historical connection, readers were forced to accept an almost conventionless set of conventions for genre divisions. Susan Sontag and William H. Gass both rewrote the philosophic novel. With Truman Capote's *In Cold Blood* (1966) and Norman Mailer's *The White Negro* (1957), *Advertisements for Myself* (1959), *Why Are We in Vietnam?* (1967), *Miami and the Siege of Chicago* and *The Armies of the Night* (both 1968), readers relinquished the boundary between fiction and nonfiction with surprising ease. In the move to what became known as the "nonfiction novel," history reappeared; the form may have come to exist, in fact, to find a legitimate use for history as it was occurring.

Based on much of the literature published, reviewed, and included in the canon during the 1950s and the 1960s, then, it is not illogical that the classification of postmodern writing is based almost entirely on writing by white men. By the late 1960s, the category included one black writer—Ishmael Reed, for his parodic *The Free-Lance Pallbearers*, 1967, and *Yellow Back Radio Broke-Down*, 1969—but for the most part, black writers were ghettoized in the category of black writing. Influential as work by James Baldwin, LeRoi Jones (now Imamu Amiri Baraka), Malcolm X, Ernest J. Gaines, Eldridge Cleaver, Jay Wright, and George Jackson was, the formal literary categories of the 1960s did not bend to include them or their work.

Regretfully, such an impasse between the accepted literary categories and work by writers of color, or by women, still exists. No

matter how postmodern, how marked by gallows humor and dissonance, a piece of writing is, if it is written by a writer who is not a
white male, it is still relegated to some other nonmainstream category. If it is written by a woman, it probably remains written by a
woman. If it is written by a Chicano, no matter how thoroughly
postmodern it may be, it remains Latino writing.

Literary life was simpler in 1965, when this study ends, because
all the various subcategories of writing did not yet exist. Much writing by people of color was appearing in limited and highly specialized newspapers or pamphlets; much writing by women was published by feminist magazines and presses. The rich and crowded
stream of American letters that came to floodstage during the 1970s
was, then, only an incipient, if steady, trickle.

It is, however, unfair to assess writing in postwar America as
monolithic—or monolingual—or to claim that literature in the 1950s
and the early 1960s was itself as conservative as other parts of the
culture were represented as being. American letters has always been
a bit unruly, and American writing at midcentury was, for many
reasons, no different.

Notes and References

PREFACE

1. Warren I. Susman, "The Thirties," in *The Development of an American Culture*, ed. Stanley Coben and Lorman Ratner (Englewood Cliffs, N.J.: Prentice-Hall, 1970), 218.
2. David Minter, *A Cultural History of the American Novel* (New York: Cambridge University Press, 1994), 151.
3. Halford E. Luccock, *American Mirror: Social, Ethical and Religious Aspects of American Literature 1930–1940* (New York: Macmillan, 1941), 48–49.
4. See my *Modern American Novel, 1914–1945: A Critical History* (Boston: Twayne, 1989), 106–116.

CHAPTER 1

1. Frederick Lewis Allen, *The Big Change, America Transforms Itself: 1900–1950* (New York: Harper & Brothers, 1952), 145.
2. Ibid., 148.
3. Halford E. Luccock, *American Mirror*, 33–34.
4. Sherwood Anderson, *Puzzled America* (New York: Charles Scribner's Sons, 1935), ix.
5. Ibid., xiii.
6. Jack Conroy and Arna Bontemps, *They Seek a City* (New York: Doubleday, Doran, 1945), 249.
7. Meridel LeSueur, "Women on the Breadlines" and "Women Are Hungry," in her *Ripening: Selected Work, 1927–1980* (New York: Feminist Press, 1982), 137.
8. Ibid., 137.
9. Ibid., 139.
10. Ibid., 141.
11. Lewis Adamic, *My America, 1928–1938* (New York: Harper and Brothers, 1938), 294.
12. Tom Kromer, *Waiting for Nothing*, in his *Waiting for Nothing and Other Writings*, ed. Arthur D. Casciato and James L. W. West III (Athens: University of Georgia Press, 1986), 221.
13. James Rorty, *Where Life Is Better: An Unsentimental American Journey* (New York: Reynal and Hitchcock, 1936), 13.
14. Erskine Caldwell, "Rachel," in *The Complete Stories of Erskine Caldwell* (Boston: Little, Brown, 1941).
15. Erskine Caldwell, "Daughter," in *The Complete Stories*, 103.
16. Albert Maltz, "Man on the Road," in *The Strenuous Decade*, ed. Daniel Aaron and Robert Bendiner (Garden City, N.Y.: Doubleday, 1970), 245–246.

17. Nelson Algren, *Somebody in Boots* (New York: Vanguard, 1935), dedication page.

18. Jack Conroy, *The Disinherited* (New York: Covici-Friede, 1933), 12.

19. Ibid., 12.

20. Ibid., 152.

21. Ibid., 255.

22. Tom Kromer, *Waiting for Nothing*, 6.

23. Ibid., 7.

24. Ibid., 66.

25. Ibid., 128.

26. Tom Kromer, "Hungry Men," in *Waiting for Nothing*, 213.

27. Ibid., 214.

28. Theodore Dreiser, "Introduction to *Harlan Miners Speak*," in *Theodore Dreiser: A Selection of Uncollected Prose*, ed. Donald Pizer (Detroit, Mich.: Wayne State University Press, 1977), 270.

29. Ibid., 270.

30. Edmund Wilson, *The American Jitters: A Year of the Slump* (1932; reprint, Freeport, New York: Books for Libraries, 1968), 50–51.

31. Ibid., 77.

32. Ibid., 79.

33. Ruth McKenney, *Industrial Valley* (New York: Harcourt, Brace and Co., 1939), 373.

34. Robert Cantwell, *The Land of Plenty* (New York: Farrar and Rinehart, 1934), 38–39.

35. Ibid., 7.

36. Ibid., 7.

37. Ibid., 232.

38. Ibid., 368.

39. Robert Cantwell, "American Exile," in *The Nation*, 20 July 1932, 61.

40. June Howard, *Form and History in American Literary Naturalism* (Chapel Hill: University of North Carolina Press, 1985), 148.

41. Albert Halper, *The Chute* (New York: Viking, 1937), 16.

42. Ibid., 3.

43. June Howard, *Form and History*, 148.

44. Ibid., 165.

45. Albert Halper, *The Chute*, 11.

46. Ibid., 12.

47. Ibid., 29–30.

48. See John A. Salmond, *Gastonia 1929* (Chapel Hill: University of North Carolina Press, 1995).

49. Dorothy Myra Page, *Gathering Storm: A Story of the Black Belt* (USSR: International, 1932), 9.

50. Ibid., 25.

51. Ibid., 45.

52. Ibid., 30.

53. See Paula Rabinowitz, *Labor and Desire: Women's Revolutionary Fiction in Depression America* (Chapel Hill: University of North Carolina Press, 1991), 91, and Barbara Foley, *Radical Representations: Politics and Form in U.S. Proletarian Fiction, 1929–1941* (Durham: Duke University Press, 1994), 369.

54. See Barbara Foley, *Radical Representations*, 398–441.

55. Ibid., 398–402.

56. Richard H. Pells, *Radical Visions and American Dreams* (New York: Harper & Row, 1973), 1–42.

57. Ibid., 9.

58. Ibid., 195.

59. Clara Weatherwax, *Marching! Marching!* (New York: International, 1935), 14.

60. Ibid., 15.

61. Ibid., 15.

62. Ibid., 11.

63. Ibid., 97.

64. Ibid., 221.

65. Ibid., 256.

66. John Steinbeck, *In Dubious Battle* (New York: Viking, 1936), 9.

67. Jay Parini, *John Steinbeck: A Biography* (New York: Heinemann, 1994), 189.

68. Ibid., 190.

69. Albert Maltz, *The Underground Stream: An Historical Novel of a Moment in the American Winter* (Boston: Little, Brown, 1940), 3.

70. Ibid., 3.

71. Ibid., 99.

72. Ibid., 100.

73. John Steinbeck, quoted in Jay Parini, *John Steinbeck*, 192.

74. Josephine Herbst, *Rope of Gold* (1939; reprint, New York: Feminist Press, 1984), 8.

75. Ibid., 424.

76. Ibid., 429.

77. Ibid., 428.

CHAPTER 2

1. Tillie Olsen's term for an author's perspective on experiences that are not her or his own—Olsen uses it to describe Rebecca Harding Davis's middle-class, educated vision as expressed in her writings about steel workers in her 1861 "Life in the Iron Mills."

2. Constance Coiner, *Better Red: The Writing and Resistance of Tillie Olsen and Meridel LeSueur* (New York: Oxford University Press, 1995), 231.

3. James T. Farrell, *Gas-House McGinty* (Cleveland: World, 1933), 21.

4. Ibid., 21.

5. Ibid., 23.

6. Ibid., 27.

7. Ibid., 31.

8. Ibid., 94.

9. Horace Gregory, "Review of *Young Lonigan*," *The Nation*, 20 July 1932, 61.

10. Ibid., 61.

11. James T. Farrell, *Studs Lonigan* (New York: Vanguard, 1935), 409–410.

12. Ibid., 410.

13. Ibid., 410.

14. Ibid., 411.

15. Ibid., 411.

16. Barbara Foley, *Radical Representations*, 328.

17. Ibid., 328.

18. Ruth Suckow, *The Folks* (New York: Grosset & Dunlap, 1934), 726.

19. Henry Roth, *Call It Sleep* (New York: Avon, 1934), 12.

20. John Dos Passos, *The 42nd Parallel* (New York: Harper & Brothers, 1930), 81.

21. Ibid., 37.

22. William Marling, *The American Roman Noir: Hammett, Cain, and Chandler* (Athens: University of Georgia Press, 1995), ix–x.

23. Ibid., xiii.

24. Dashiell Hammett, *The Maltese Falcon*, in *The Novels of Dashiell Hammett* (New York: Alfred A. Knopf, 1965), 436.

25. James M. Cain, *The Postman Always Rings Twice*, in *Cain x 3* (New York: Alfred A. Knopf, 1969), 9.

26. Ibid., 13.

27. Ibid., 36.

28. James M. Cain, *Double Indemnity*, in *Cain x 3*, 387.

29. Ibid., 403.

30. Ibid., 434–435.

31. Ibid., 464.

32. Raymond Chandler, *Farewell, My Lovely*, in *The Raymond Chandler Omnibus* (New York: Alfred A. Knopf, 1964), 242.

33. Ibid., 313.

34. David Minter, *A Cultural History of the American Novel*, 168.

35. Paula Rabinowitz, "Women and U.S. Literary Radicalism," in *Writing Red*, ed. Charlotte Nekola and Paula Rabinowitz (New York: Feminist Press, 1987), 13.

36. Winifred D. Wandersee, "The Economics of Middle-Income Family Life: Working Women during the Great Depression," in *Decades of Discontent: The Women's Movement, 1920–1940*, ed. Lois Scharf and Joan M. Jensen (Westport, Conn.: Greenwood Press, 1983), 54.

37. Tillie Olsen, *Yonnondio: From the Thirties* (New York: Dell, 1974), 117.

38. Ibid., 10.

39. Josephine Johnson, *Now in November* (New York: Simon & Schuster, 1934), 3.

40. Ibid., 226.

41. Ibid., 230.

42. Caroline Slade, *The Triumph of Willie Pond* (New York: Vanguard, 1940), 117.

43. Ibid., 362.

44. Tess Slesinger, *The Unpossessed* (New York: Simon & Schuster, 1934), 4.

45. Richard Wright, introduction to Nelson Algren, *Never Come Morning* (New York: Harper and Brothers, 1942), x.

46. Nelson Algren, *Never Come Morning*, 284.

CHAPTER 3

1. Albert Halper, *Sons of the Fathers* (New York: Harper and Brothers, 1940), 383.

2. Ibid., 423.

3. Richard H. Pells, *Radical Visions and American Dreams*, 327.

4. Ibid., 327.

5. Ibid., 329.

6. Robert Penn Warren, *All the King's Men* (New York: Random House, 1946), v.

7. Ibid., ii.

8. Ibid., 3.

9. Ibid., 462.

10. Chester E. Eisinger, *Fiction of the Forties* (Chicago: University of Chicago Press, 1963), 27.

11. Ibid., 27.

12. Ibid., 27.

13. Joseph J. Waldmeir, *American Novels of the Second World War* (The Hague: Mouton, 1969), 115.

14. Robert C. Healey, "Novelists of the War: A Bunch of Dispossessed," in *Fifty Years of the American Novel, 1900–1950*, ed. Harold C. Gardiner, S. J. (New York: Charles Scribner's Sons, 1951), 259.

15. Irwin Shaw, *The Young Lions* (New York: Random House, 1948), 21.

16. Ibid., 22.

17. Robert C. Healey, "Novelists of the War," 264.

18. William Styron, *The Long March* (New York: Random House, 1952), 3.

19. Ibid., 109.

20. Ibid., 109.

21. Herman Wouk, *The Caine Mutiny* (Garden City, N.Y.: Doubleday, 1951), 448.

22. Ibid., 446.

23. Peter G. Jones, *War and the Novelist* (Columbia: University of Missouri Press, 1976), 12.

24. Ibid., 44.

25. John Hersey, *The War Lover* (New York: Alfred A. Knopf, 1959), 4.

26. Ibid., 3–4.

27. Saul Bellow, *Dangling Man* (New York: Vanguard, 1944), 18.

28. Ibid., 30.

29. Ibid., 57.

30. Ibid., 78.

31. Ibid., 81.

32. Ibid., 81.

33. Ibid., 82.

34. The title of Bellow's second novel (1947), in which Asa Leventhal enacts the victimhood of the Jew in a largely anti-Semitic culture.

35. Ibid., 84.

36. Ibid., 191.

37. Ibid., 166.
38. Paul Bowles, *The Sheltering Sky* (New York: New Directions, 1949), 11.
39. Ibid., 14.
40. Ibid., 23.
41. Ibid., 307.
42. John Updike, *Rabbit, Run* (New York: Alfred A. Knopf, 1960), 136.
43. Ibid., 166.
44. Walker Percy, *The Moviegoer* (New York: Alfred A. Knopf, 1960), 40.
45. Ibid., 52.
46. Ibid., 71.
47. Ibid., 118.
48. Ibid., 127, 165.
49. Ibid., 18.
50. Ibid., 75.
51. Ibid., 83.
52. John Updike, *Rabbit, Run*, 172.
53. Walker Percy, *The Moviegoer*, 52.
54. Ibid., 52–53.

CHAPTER 4

1. Christopher Lasch, *The New Radicalism in America, 1889–1963: The Intellectual as a Social Type* (New York: Vintage, 1967), 327.
2. Granville Hicks, "The Fighting Decade," in *The Strenuous Decade*, ed. Daniel Aaron and Robert Bendiner (Garden City, N.Y.: Doubleday (Anchor), 1970), 513.
3. Christopher Lasch, *New Radicalism*, 333.
4. Granville Hicks, "Fighting Decade," 514.
5. Christopher Lasch, *New Radicalism*, 316.
6. Nelson Algren, *The Man with the Golden Arm* (Garden City, N.Y.: Doubleday, 1949), 181.
7. Ibid., 156.
8. Wallace Stegner, *The Big Rock Candy Mountain* (New York: Duell, Sloan, and Pearce, 1943), 57.
9. Ibid., 140–141.
10. Chester E. Eisinger, *Fiction of the Forties*, 231.
11. Truman Capote, *Other Voices, Other Rooms* (New York: Random House, 1948), 4.
12. Ibid., 74.
13. Ibid., 137.
14. Ibid., 100.
15. Ibid., 207.
16. Gore Vidal, *The City and the Pillar* (New York: E. P. Dutton, 1948), 47–49.
17. Ibid., 11.
18. Ibid., 11.
19. John Updike, "The 50s: Each Man Was an Island," *Newsweek*, 3 January 1994, 36–37.

20. Carson McCullers, *Reflections in a Golden Eye* (Boston: Houghton Mifflin, 1941), 13.
21. Ibid., 124.
22. Ibid., 156.
23. John W. Aldridge, *After the Lost Generation* (New York: Farrar, Straus, & Giroux, 1951), 196.

CHAPTER 5

1. Review of *Invisible Man*, *Publishers' Weekly* (1952), 161:1303.
2. Laura Doyle, *Bordering on the Body: The Racial Matrix of Modern Fiction and Culture* (New York: Oxford University Press, 1994), 174.
3. Ibid., 175.
4. James Baldwin, *Giovanni's Room* (New York: Dial, 1956), 100.
5. Ibid., 122.
6. Ibid., 120.
7. Ibid., 110.
8. See Janice Radway, *Reading the Romance* (Chapel Hill: University of North Carolina Press, 1984), and Andrew Ross, *No Respect: Intellectuals and Popular Culture* (New York: Routledge, 1989).
9. Elizabeth Long, *The American Dream and the Popular Novel* (Boston: Routledge & Kegan Paul, 1985), 3–4.
10. Ibid., 8.
11. Chester E. Eisinger, *Fiction of the Forties*, 129.
12. Quoted in "The Novels of the Second World War," *Publishers' Weekly*, September–October 1948, 1031.
13. Margaret Anne O'Connor, "Flannery O'Connor," in *The Oxford Companion to Women's Writing in the United States*, ed. Cathy N. Davidson and Linda Wagner-Martin (New York: Oxford University Press, 1995), 641.
14. Ibid., 641.
15. Jean Stafford, *Boston Adventure* (New York: Harcourt, Brace, 1944), 3.
16. Jean Stafford, *The Mountain Lion* (New York: Harcourt, Brace, 1947), 228.
17. John Updike, "The 50s: Each Man Was an Island," *Newsweek*, 3 January 1994, 36.

CHAPTER 6

1. Ihab H. Hassan, *Radical Innocence* (Princeton, N.J.: Princeton University Press, 1961), 61.
2. Ibid., 259–260.
3. Ihab H. Hassan, *Contemporary American Literature, 1945–1972: An Introduction* (New York: Frederick Ungar, 1973), 43.
4. J. D. Salinger, *The Catcher in the Rye* (Boston: Little, Brown, 1951), 173.
5. Ibid., 88.
6. Ibid., 165.
7. Kay Boyle, "A Declaration for 1955," in *Words That Must Somehow Be Said: Selected Essays*, ed. Elizabeth S. Bell (San Francisco: North Point, 1985), 62.

8. Ibid., 62.
9. Ibid., 65.
10. Ihab H. Hassan, *Radical Innocence*, 286.
11. Bernard Bergonzi, *The Situation of the Novel* (London: Macmillan, 1970), 85.
12. Ibid., 86.
13. Frederick R. Karl, *American Fictions, 1940–1980* (New York: Harper & Row, 1983), 158.
14. Ibid., 158.
15. Andreas Huyssen, *After the Great Divide: Modernism, Mass Culture, Postmodernism* (Bloomington: Indiana University Press, 1986), 184, 189.
16. Ibid., 189.
17. Leslie A. Fiedler, "John Barth: An Eccentric Genius," in *On Contemporary Literature*, ed. Richard Kostelanetz (New York: Avon, 1964), 239.
18. Ibid., 241.
19. Ibid., 241.
20. John Barth, *The Sot-Weed Factor* (New York: Grosset & Dunlop, 1960), 344–345.
21. Ibid., 804.
22. John Barth, "The Literature of Exhaustion," in *The American Novel since World War II*, ed. Marcus Klein (Greenwich, Conn.: Fawcett, 1969), 267.
23. Ibid., 269.
24. Ibid., 269.
25. John Hawkes, "Notes on the Wild Goose Chase," in *The American Novel since World War II*, ed. Marcus Klein (Greenwich, Conn.: Fawcett, 1969), 250.
26. Ibid., 250.
27. Saul Bellow, "Some Notes on Recent American Fiction," in *The American Novel since World War II*, ed. Marcus Klein (Greenwich, Conn.: Fawcett, 1969), 171.
28. Ibid., 171.
29. Ibid., 174.
30. John Hawkes, *Second Skin* (New York: New Directions, 1964), 1.
31. Ihab H. Hassan, *Contemporary American Literature*, 52.
32. John Hawkes, *Second Skin*, 157.
33. Ibid., 148–149.
34. Ibid., 158.
35. Ibid., 159.
36. Saul Bellow, *Henderson the Rain King* (New York: Viking, 1959), 90–91.
37. Ibid., 113.
38. Ibid., 106.
39. Ibid., 107.
40. Bruce Bawer, *Diminishing Fictions* (St. Paul, Minn.: Graywolf, 1988), 207.
41. Burton Feldman, "Anatomy of Black Humor," in *The American Novel since World War II*, 224.
42. Ibid., 224.

43. Ibid., 224–225.
44. Joseph Heller, *Catch-22* (New York: Simon & Schuster, 1961), 87.
45. Eric Homberger, "United States," in *The Second World War in Fiction*, ed. Holger Klein (London: Macmillan, 1984), 204–205.
46. Joseph Heller, *Catch-22*, 242.
47. Ibid., 242.
48. Frederick R. Karl, *American Fictions, 1940–1980*, 310.
49. Joseph Heller, *Catch-22*, 442.
50. Eric Homberger, "United States," 174.
51. Peter G. Jones, *War and the Novelist* (Columbia: University of Missouri Press, 1976), 203.
52. Kurt Vonnegut Jr., *The Sirens of Titan* (London: Victor Gollancz, 1959), 7.
53. Ibid., 7.
54. Kurt Vonnegut Jr., *Cat's Cradle* (New York: Holt, Rinehart and Winston, 1963), 114.
55. Richard Kostelanetz, introduction to his *On Contemporary Literature* (New York: Avon, 1964), xxv.

POSTSCRIPT

1. Eric Homberger, "United States," in *The Second World War in Fiction*, ed. Holger Klein (London: Macmillan, 1984), 200, 202.
2. Ihab H. Hassan, "The Character of Post-War Fiction in America," in *On Contemporary Literature*, ed. Richard Kostelanetz (New York: Avon, 1964), 41–42.

Selected Bibliography

Aaron, Daniel. *Writers on the Left: Episodes in American Literary Communism.* New York: Harcourt, Brace & World, 1961.

Aaron, Daniel, and Robert Bendiner, eds. *The Strenuous Decade: A Social and Intellectual Record of the Nineteen-Thirties.* Garden City, N.Y.: Doubleday (Anchor), 1970.

Adamic, Lewis. *My America, 1928–1938.* New York: Harper and Brothers, 1938.

Aldridge, John W. *After the Lost Generation.* New York: Farrar, Straus, & Giroux, 1951.

Algren, Nelson. *The Man with the Golden Arm.* Garden City, N.Y.: Doubleday, 1949.

———. *Never Come Morning.* New York: Harper and Brothers, 1942.

———. *Somebody in Boots.* New York: Vanguard, 1935.

Allen, Frederick Lewis. *The Big Change, America Transforms Itself: 1900–1950.* New York: Harper & Brothers, 1952.

Anderson, Sherwood. *Puzzled America.* New York: Charles Scribner's Sons, 1935.

———. *Winesburg, Ohio.* New York: Huebsch, 1919.

Arnow, Harriette. *The Dollmaker.* New York: Macmillan, 1954.

———. *Hunter's Horn.* New York: Avon, 1949.

Attaway, William. *Blood on the Forge.* New York: Doubleday, Doran, 1941.

———. *Let Me Breathe Thunder.* New York: Doubleday, Doran, 1939.

Baldwin, James. *Giovanni's Room.* New York: Dial, 1956.

———. *Go Tell It on the Mountain.* Garden City, N.Y.: Doubleday, 1953.

Barth, John. *The End of the Road.* Garden City, N.Y.: Doubleday, 1958.

———. *The Floating Opera.* New York: Appleton-Century-Crofts, 1956.

———. *Giles Goat-Boy, or The Revised New Syllabus.* Garden City, N.Y.: Doubleday, 1966.

———. "The Literature of Exhaustion." In *The American Novel since World War II,* edited by Marcus Klein, 267–279. Greenwich, Conn.: Fawcett, 1969.

———. "The Literature of Replenishment." *Atlantic Monthly,* January 1980, 65–71.

———. *Lost in the Funhouse.* Garden City, N.Y.: Doubleday, 1968.

———. *The Sot-Weed Factor.* New York: Grosset & Dunlap, 1960.

Barthelme, Donald. *Snow White.* New York: Atheneum, 1967.

Bawer, Bruce. *Diminishing Fictions.* St. Paul, Minn.: Graywolf, 1988.

Beach, Joseph Warren. *American Fiction, 1920–1940.* New York: Russell & Russell, 1960.

Bellow, Saul. *The Adventures of Augie March.* New York: Viking, 1953.

———. *Dangling Man.* New York: Vanguard, 1944.

———. *Henderson the Rain King.* New York: Viking, 1959.

———. *Seize the Day.* New York: Viking, 1961.

————. "Some Notes on Recent American Fiction." In *The American Novel since World War II*, edited by Marcus Klein, 159–174. Greenwich, Conn.: Fawcett, 1969.

————. *The Victim*. New York: Vanguard: 1947.

Bergonzi, Bernard. *The Situation of the Novel*. London: Macmillan, 1970.

Blyth, LeGette. *Bold Galilean*. Chapel Hill: University of North Carolina Press, 1948.

Borges, Jorge Luis. "Pierre Menard, Author of Don Quixote." In *Ficciones*, 58–66. London: Harrap, 1956.

Bowles, Paul. *The Sheltering Sky*. New York: New Directions, 1949.

Boyle, Kay. "A Declaration for 1955." In *Words That Must Somehow Be Said: Selected Essays*, edited by Elizabeth S. Bell, 60–66. San Francisco: North Point, 1985.

Brooks, Gwendolyn. *Annie Allen, Poems*. New York: Harper, 1949.

————. *Maud Martha, A Novel*. New York: Harper, 1953.

————. *A Street in Bronzeville*. New York: Harper and Brothers, 1945.

Cain, James M. *Double Indemnity*. In *Cain x 3*, 363–465. New York: Alfred A. Knopf, 1969.

————. *The Postman Always Rings Twice*. In *Cain x 3*, 1–101. New York: Alfred A. Knopf, 1969.

Caldwell, Erskine. "Daughter." In *The Complete Stories of Erskine Caldwell*, 235–240. Boston: Little, Brown, 1941.

————. *God's Little Acre*. New York: Penguin, 1933.

————. "Rachel." In *The Complete Stories of Erskine Caldwell*, 269–277. Boston: Little, Brown, 1941.

————. *Tobacco Road*. In *Three by Caldwell*, 1–241. Boston: Little, Brown, 1932.

Camus, Albert. *The Stranger*. New York: Alfred A. Knopf, 1946.

Cantwell, Robert. "American Exile." *The Nation*, 20 July 1932, 61.

————. *The Land of Plenty*. New York: Farrar and Rinehart, 1934.

Capote, Truman. *In Cold Blood*. New York: Random House, 1965.

————. *Other Voices, Other Rooms*. New York: Random House, 1948.

Carby, Hazel. *Reconstructing Womanhood: The Emergence of the Afro-American Woman Novelist*. New York: Oxford University Press, 1989.

Caregie, Dale. *How to Stop Worrying and Start Living*. New York: Simon & Schuster, 1948.

Chandler, Raymond. *The Big Sleep*. In *The Raymond Chandler Omnibus*, 1–139. New York: Alfred A. Knopf, 1964.

————. *Farewell, My Lovely*. In *The Raymond Chandler Omnibus*, 141–315. New York: Alfred A. Knopf, 1964.

Chase, Mary Ellen. *The Lovely Ambition*. New York: Norton, 1960.

Coiner, Constance. *Better Red: The Writing and Resistance of Tillie Olsen and Meridel LeSueur*. New York: Oxford University Press, 1995.

————. "Class, 1930s Proletarian Writing." In *The Oxford Companion to Women's Writing in the United States*, edited by Cathy N. Davidson and Linda Wagner-Martin, 193–197. New York: Oxford University Press, 1994.

Conroy, Jack. *The Disinherited*. New York: Covici-Friede, 1933.

Conroy, Jack, and Arna Bontemps. *They Seek a City.* New York: Doubleday, Doran, 1945.
Conroy, Jack, and Curt Johnson, eds. *Writers in Revolt: The Anvil Anthology, 1933–1940.* Westport, Conn.: Lawrence Hill, 1973.
Costain, Thomas. *The Moneyman.* Garden City, N.Y.: Doubleday, 1947.
Cozzens, James Gould. *Guard of Honor.* New York: Harcourt, Brace, 1948.
Didion, Joan. *A Book of Common Prayer.* New York: Simon & Schuster, 1977.
———. *Play It as It Lays.* London: Weidenfeld & Nicolson, 1990.
———. *Run River.* New York: I. Obolensky, 1963.
Di Donato, Pietro. *Christ in Concrete.* Chicago: Esquire, 1937.
Donleavy, J. P. *The Ginger Man.* New York: McDowell, Obolensky, 1958.
Dos Passos, John. *The 42nd Parallel.* New York: Harper & Brothers, 1930. Also in *U.S.A.* New York: Harcourt, Brace, 1937.
———. *Midcentury.* Boston: Houghton Mifflin, 1961.
Douglas, Ann. *Terrible Honesty: Mongrel Manhattan in the 1920s.* New York: Farrar, Straus & Giroux, 1995.
Doyle, Laura. *Bordering on the Body: The Racial Matrix of Modern Fiction and Culture.* New York: Oxford University Press, 1994.
Dreiser, Theodore. "Introduction to *Harlan Miners Speak.*" In *Theodore Dreiser: A Selection of Uncollected Prose,* edited by Donald Pizer, 265–271. Detroit, Mich.: Wayne State University Press, 1977.
du Maurier, Dame Daphne. *My Cousin, Rachel.* Garden City, N.Y.: Doubleday, 1952.
Eisinger, Chester E. *Fiction of the Forties.* Chicago: University of Chicago Press, 1963.
Ellison, Ralph. *Invisible Man.* New York: Modern Library, 1952.
Erikson, Eric. *Childhood and Society.* New York: Norton, 1950.
Farrell, James T. *Gas-House McGinty.* Cleveland: World, 1933.
———. *Studs Lonigan: A Trilogy.* New York: Vanguard, 1935.
Faulkner, William. *Absalom, Absalom!* New York: Random House, 1936.
———. *A Fable.* New York: Random House, 1954.
———. *The Reivers.* New York: Random House, 1962.
Feldman, Burton. "Anatomy of Black Humor." In *The American Novel since World War II,* edited by Marcus Klein, 224–228. Greenwich, Conn.: Fawcett, 1969.
Ferber, Edna. *Giant.* Garden City, N.Y.: Doubleday, 1952.
———. *Ice Palace.* Garden City, N.Y.: Doubleday, 1958.
Fiedler, Leslie A. "John Barth: An Eccentric Genius." In *On Contemporary Literature,* edited by Richard Kostelanetz, 238–243. New York: Avon, 1964.
———. *Love and Death in the American Novel.* New York: Stein & Day, 1960.
Fitzgerald, F. Scott. *The Great Gatsby.* New York: Scribner's, 1925.
———. *The Last Tycoon.* New York: Scribner's, 1941.
———. *Tender is the Night.* New York: Scribner's, 1934.
Foley, Barbara. *Radical Representations: Politics and Form in U.S. Proletarian Fiction, 1929–1941.* Durham: Duke University Press, 1994.
Friedan, Betty. *The Feminine Mystique.* New York: Norton, 1963.
Friedman, Bruce J. *Stern.* New York: Simon & Schuster, 1962.

Gaddis, William. *The Recognitions.* New York: Harcourt, Brace Jovanovich, 1952.

Gass, William H. *Omensetter's Luck.* New York: New American Library, 1966.

Gellhorn, Martha. *The Wine of Astonishment.* 1948. Reprinted as *Point of No Return,* New York: Plume, 1989.

Ginsberg, Allen. *Howl and Other Poems.* San Fransisco: City Lights, 1956.

Glasgow, Ellen. *A Certain Measure: An Interpretation of Prose Fiction.* New York: Harcourt, Brace and Co., 1943.

———. *In This Our Life.* New York: Harcourt, Brace and Co., 1941.

———. *The Woman Within.* New York: Harcourt, Brace and Co., 1954.

Gordon, Caroline. *Aleck Maury, Sportsman.* New York: Scribner's, 1934.

———. *Green Centuries.* New York: Scribner's, 1941.

———. *None Shall Look Back.* New York: Scribner's, 1937

———. *Penhally.* New York: Scribner's, 1931.

———. *The Women on the Porch.* New York: Scribner's, 1944.

Gregory, Horace, "Review of *Young Lonigan.*" *The Nation,* 20 July 1932, 61.

Hailey, Arthur. *Hotel.* Garden City, N.Y.: Doubleday, 1965.

Halper, Albert. *The Chute.* New York: Viking, 1937.

———. *Sons of the Fathers.* New York: Harper & Brothers, 1940.

Hammett, Dashiell. *The Maltese Falcon.* In *The Novels of Dashiell Hammett,* 293–440. New York: Alfred A. Knopf, 1965.

Hansberry, Lorraine. *A Raisin in the Sun.* New York: Random House, 1959.

Hart, James D. *The Popular Book.* New York: Oxford University Press, 1950.

Hassan, Ihab H. "The Character of Post-War Fiction in America." In *On Contemporary Literature,* edited by Richard Kostelanetz, 36–47. New York: Avon, 1964.

———. *Contemporary American Literature, 1945–1972: An Introduction.* New York: Frederick Ungar, 1973.

———. *Radical Innocence: Studies in the Contemporary American Novel.* New York: Harper & Row, 1961.

———. *The Beetle Leg.* New York: New Directions, 1951.

———. *The Cannibal.* New York: New Directions, 1949.

Hawkes, John. *The Lime Twig.* New York: New Directions, 1961.

———. "Notes on the Wild Goose Chase." In *The American Novel since World War II,* edited by Marcus Klein, 247–251. Greenwich, Conn.: Fawcett, 1969.

———. *Second Skin.* New York: New Directions, 1964.

Hawley, Cameron. *Cash McCall.* Boston: Houghton Mifflin, 1955.

Healey, Robert C. "Novelists of the War: A Bunch of Dispossessed." In *Fifty Years of the American Novel, 1900–1950,* edited by Harold C. Gardiner, S.J., 257–271. New York: Charles Scribner's Sons, 1951.

Heller, Joseph. *Catch-22.* New York: Simon & Schuster, 1961.

Hemingway, Ernest. *Across the River and into the Trees.* New York: Scribner's, 1950

———. *The Old Man and the Sea.* New York: Scribner's, 1952.

———. *The Sun Also Rises.* New York: Scribner's, 1926.

Herbst, Josephine. *Rope of Gold.* 1939. Reprint, New York: Feminist Press, 1984.

Hersey, John. *A Bell for Adano*. New York: Alfred A. Knopf, 1944.

———. *Hiroshima*. New York: Alfred A. Knopf, 1946.

———. *Into the Valley*. New York: Alfred A. Knopf, 1943.

———. *Men on Bataan*. New York: Alfred A. Knopf, 1942.

———. *The Wall*. New York: Alfred A. Knopf, 1961.

———. *The War Lover*. New York: Alfred A. Knopf, 1959.

Hicks, Granville. "The Fighting Decade." In *The Strenuous Decade*, edited by Daniel Aaron and Robert Bendiner, 505–515. Garden City, N.Y.: Doubleday (Anchor), 1970.

Himes, Chester. *Cotton Comes to Harlem*. New York: Putnam, 1965.

———. *The Crazy Kill*. Chatham, N.Y.: The Chatham Bookseller, 1959.

———. *For Love of Imabelle* (retitled *A Rage in Harlem*). London: Allison & Busby, 1957.

———. *If He Hollers Let Him Go*. New York: Thunder's Mouth Press, 1986.

Hobson, Laura Z. *Gentlemen's Agreement*. New York: Simon & Schuster, 1947.

Homberger, Eric. *American Writers and Radical Politics, 1900–1939*. New York: St. Martin's, 1986.

———. "United States." In *The Second World War in Fiction*, edited by Holger Klein, 173–205. London: Macmillan, 1984.

Howard, June. *Form and History in American Literary Naturalism*. Chapel Hill: University of North Carolina Press, 1985.

Huyssen, Andreas. *After the Great Divide: Modernism, Mass Culture, Postmodernism*. Bloomington: Indiana University Press, 1986.

Jackson, Shirley. *The Bird's Nest*. New York: Farrar, Straus, and Young, 1954.

———. *Hangsaman*. New York: Ace, 1951.

———. *The Haunting of Hill House*. New York: Viking, 1959.

———. *Life Among the Savages*. New York: Farrar, Straus, and Young, 1953.

———. *The Lottery*. New York: Farrar, Straus, 1949.

———. *Raising Demons*. New York: Farrar, Straus and Cudahy, 1957.

———. *We Have Always Lived in the Castle*. New York: Viking, 1962.

Jarrell, Randall. *Pictures from an Institution*. New York: Alfred A. Knopf, 1954.

Johnson, Josephine. *Now in November*. New York: Simon & Schuster, 1934.

Jones, James. *From Here to Eternity*. New York: Charles Scribner's Sons, 1951.

Jones, Peter G. *War and the Novelist*. Columbia: University of Missouri Press, 1976.

Kalaidjian, Walter. *American Culture between the Wars: Revisionary Modernism and Postmodern Critique*. New York: Columbia University Press, 1993.

Karl, Frederick R. *American Fictions, 1940–1980*. New York: Harper & Row, 1983.

Kerouac, Jack. *On the Road*. New York: New American Library, 1957.

Kesey, Ken. *One Flew Over the Cuckoo's Nest*. New York: Viking, 1962.

Keyes, Francis Parkinson. *Came a Cavalier*. New York: J. Messner, 1947.

Killens, John O. *And Then We Heard the Thunder*. New York: Alfred A. Knopf, 1963.

Kinsey, Alfred C. *Sexual Behavior in the Human Male*. Philadelphia: W. B. Saunders, 1948.

Klein, Marcus. *After Alienation*. Cleveland: World, 1964.

Klein, Marcus, ed. *The American Novel since World War II.* Greenwich, Conn.: Fawcett, 1969.

Klinkowitz, Jerome. *The American 1960s: Imaginative Arts in a Decade of Change.* Ames: Iowa State University Press, 1980.

Kostelanetz, Richard, ed. *On Contemporary Literature.* New York: Avon, 1964.

Kromer, Tom. *Waiting for Nothing.* In *Waiting for Nothing and Other Writings,* edited by Arthur D. Casciato and James L. W. West III, 1–129. Athens: University of Georgia Press, 1986.

———. "Hungry Men." In *Waiting for Nothing and Other Writings,* edited by Arthur D. Casciato and James L. W. West III, 213–215. Athens: University of Georgia Press, 1986.

Lasch, Christopher. *The New Radicalism in America, 1889–1963: The Intellectual as a Social Type.* New York: Vintage, 1967.

LeSueur, Meridel. "Women on the Breadlines." In her *Ripening: Selected Work, 1927–1980,* edited by Elaine Hedges, 137–143. New York: Feminist Press, 1982.

———. "Women Are Hungry." In her *Ripening: Selected Work, 1927–1980,* edited by Elaine Hedges, 144–157. New York: Feminist Press, 1982.

Lewis, Sinclair. *It Can't Happen Here.* Garden City, N.Y.: Doubleday, 1935.

Long, Elizabeth. *The American Dream and the Popular Novel.* Boston: Routledge & Kegan Paul, 1985.

Luccock, Halford E. *American Mirror: Social, Ethical and Religious Aspects of American Literature 1930–1940.* New York: Macmillan, 1941.

Madden, David, ed. *Proletarian Writers of the Thirties.* Carbondale: Southern Illinois University Press, 1968.

Mailer, Norman. *Advertisements for Myself.* New York: Putnam, 1959.

———. *The Armies of the Night.* New York: New American Library, 1968.

———. *Miami and the Siege of Chicago.* New York: New American Library, 1968.

———. *The Naked and the Dead.* New York: Rinehart, 1948.

———. *The White Negro.* San Francisco: City Lights Books, 1957.

———. *Why Are We in Vietnam?* New York: Putnam, 1967.

Maltz, Albert. *The Cross and the Arrow.* New York: Book Find Club, 1944.

———. "Man on the Road." In *The Strenuous Decade,* edited by Daniel Aaron and Robert Bendiner, Document 31, "A Chapter from the Annals of the Poor," 239–248. Garden City, N.Y.: Doubleday (Anchor), 1970.

———. *The Underground Stream: An Historical Novel of a Moment in the American Winter.* Boston: Little, Brown, 1940.

Marling, William. *The American Roman Noir: Hammett, Cain, and Chandler.* Athens: University of Georgia Press, 1995.

Marshall, Catherine. *A Man Called Peter: The Story of Peter Marshall.* New York: McGraw-Hill, 1951.

Marshall, Paule. *Brown Girl, Brownstones.* New York: Random House, 1959.

McCarthy, Mary. *The Company She Keeps.* New York: Harcourt, Brace, 1942.

———. *The Group.* New York: Harcourt, Brace, and World, 1963.

McCullers, Carson. *The Heart Is a Lonely Hunter.* Boston: Houghton Mifflin, 1940.

———. *The Member of the Wedding.* Boston: Houghton Mifflin, 1946.

———. *Reflections in a Golden Eye*. Boston: Houghton Mifflin, 1941.
McKenney, Ruth. *Industrial Valley*. New York: Harcourt, Brace, and Co., 1939.
Metalious, Grace. *Peyton Place*. New York: Messner, 1956.
Miller, Henry. *The Tropic of Cancer*. Paris: Obelisk, 1957.
———. *The Tropic of Capricorn*. Paris: Obelisk, 1957.
Michener, James. *Hawaii*. New York: Random House, 1959.
Mills, C. Wright. *The Power Elite*. New York: Oxford University Press, 1956.
Minter, David. *A Cultural History of the American Novel*. New York: Cambridge University Press, 1994.
Mitchell, Margaret. *Gone With the Wind*. New York: Macmillan, 1936.
Motley, Willard. *Knock on Any Door*. New York: D. Appleton-Century, 1947.
———. *Let No Man Write My Epitaph*. New York: Random House, 1958.
Nabokov, Vladimir. *Ada*. New York: McGraw-Hill, 1969.
———. *Lolita*. New York: Putnam, 1955
———. *Pale Fire*. New York: Putnam, 1962.
———. *Prin*. Garden City, N.Y.: Doubleday, 1957.
Naison, Mark. *Communists in Harlem during the Depression*. New York: Grove Press, 1983.
Nekola, Charlotte and Paula Rabinowitz, eds. *Writing Red: An Anthology of American Women Writers, 1930–1940*. New York: Feminist Press, 1987.
Nelson, Cary. *Repression and Recovery: Modern American Poetry and the Politics of Cultural Memory, 1910–1945*. Madison: University of Wisconsin Press, 1989.
Niggli, Josefina. *Mexican Village*. Chapel Hill: University of North Carolina Press, 1945.
———. *Step Down, Elder Brother*. New York: Rinehart, 1947.
"The Novels of the Second World War." *Publishers' Weekly*, September–October 1948, 1802–1808.
Oates, Joyce Carol. *Expensive People*. New York: Vanguard, 1968.
———. *A Garden of Earthly Delights*. New York: Vanguard, 1967.
———. *them*. New York: Vanguard, 1969.
———. *With Shuddering Fall*. New York: Vanguard, 1964.
O'Connor, Flannery. *Everything that Rises Must Converge*. New York: Farrar, Straus, & Giroux, 1965.
———. *A Good Man is Hard to Find and Other Stories*. New York: Harcourt, Brace, 1955.
———. *Wise Blood*. New York: Harcourt, Brace, 1952.
———. *The Violent Bear It Away*. New York: Farrar, Straus & Cudahy, 1960.
O'Connor, Margaret Anne. "Flannery O'Connor." In *The Oxford Companion to Women's Writing in the United States*, edited by Cathy N. Davidson and Linda Wagner-Martin, 641–642. New York: Oxford University Press, 1995.
Okada, John. *No-No Boy*. Seattle: University of Washington Press, 1957.
Olsen, Tillie. *Yonnondio: From the Thirties*. New York: Dell, 1974.
Page, Dorothy Myra. *Gathering Storm: A Story of the Black Belt*. USSR: International, 1932.
Parini, Jay. *John Steinbeck: A Biography*. New York: Heinemann, 1994.

Peeler, David P. *Hope among Us Yet, Social Criticism and Social Solace in Depression America.* Athens: University of Georgia Press, 1987.

Pells, Richard H. *Radical Visions and American Dreams.* New York: Harper & Row, 1973.

Percy, Walker. *The Moviegoer.* New York: Alfred A. Knopf, 1960.

Petry, Ann. *The Street.* Boston: Houghton Mifflin, 1946.

Plath, Sylvia. *The Bell Jar.* 1963. Reprint, New York: Harper & Row, 1972.

Pynchon, Thomas. *The Crying of Lot 49.* Philadelphia: Lippincott, 1966.

———. *V.* Philadelphia: Lippincott, 1963.

Rabinowitz, Paula. *Labor and Desire: Women's Revolutionary Fiction in Depression America.* Chapel Hill: University of North Carolina Press, 1991.

———. "Women and U.S. Literary Radicalism." In *Writing Red: An Anthology of American Women Writers,* edited by Charlotte Nekola and Paula Rabinowitz, 1–16. New York: Feminist Press, 1987.

Radway, Janice. *Reading the Romance.* Chapel Hill: University of North Carolina Press, 1984.

Rand, Ayn. *Atlas Shrugged.* New York: Random House, 1957.

Reed, Ishmael. *The Free-Lance Pallbearers.* New York: Atheneum, 1967.

———. *Yellow Back Radio Broke-Down.* Chatham, N.Y.: Chatham Bookseller, 1969.

Rideout, Walter B. *The Radical Novel in the United States, 1900–1954: Some Interrelations of Literature and Society.* Cambridge: Harvard University Press, 1956.

Riesman, David, with Nathan Glazer and R. Denny. *The Lonely Crowd.* New Haven, Conn.: Yale University Press, 1961.

Robbins, Harold. *The Carpetbaggers.* New York: Simon & Schuster, 1961.

Rollins, William, Jr. *The Wall of Men.* Concord, New Hampshire: Modern Age, 1938.

Rorty, James. *Where Life Is Better: An Unsentimental American Journey.* New York: Reynal and Hitchcock, 1936.

Ross, Andrew. *No Respect: Intellectuals and Popular Culture.* New York: Routledge, 1989.

Roth, Henry. *Call It Sleep.* New York: Avon, 1934.

Roth, Philip. *Goodbye, Columbus and Five Short Stories.* Boston: Houghton Mifflin, 1959.

Ruark, Robert. *Something of Value.* Garden City, N.Y.: Doubleday, 1955.

Salinger, J. D. *The Catcher in the Rye.* Boston: Little, Brown, 1951.

———. "A Perfect Day for Bananafish." In *Nine Stories,* 7–18. Boston: Little, Brown, 1954.

Salmond, John A. *Gastonia 1929.* Chapel Hill: University of North Carolina Press, 1995.

Shaw, Irwin. *The Young Lions.* New York: Random House, 1948.

Slade, Caroline. *The Triumph of Willie Pond.* New York: Vanguard, 1940.

Slesinger, Tess. *The Unpossessed.* New York: Simon & Schuster, 1934.

Smith, Betty. *Tomorrow Will Be Better.* New York: Harper, 1948.

———. *A Tree Grows in Brooklyn.* New York: Harper and Brothers, 1943.

Smith, Lillian. *Strange Fruit.* New York: Reynal & Hitchcock, 1944.

Spencer, Elizabeth. *The Light in the Piazza.* New York: McGraw-Hill, 1960.
———. *This Crooked Way.* New York: Dodd, Mead, 1952.
———. *The Voice at the Back Door.* New York: McGraw-Hill, 1956.
Stafford, Jean. *Boston Adventure.* New York: Harcourt, Brace, 1944.
———. *The Mountain Lion.* New York: Harcourt, Brace, 1947.
Stegner, Wallace. *The Big Rock Candy Mountain.* New York: Duell, Sloan & Pearce, 1943.
Stein, Gertrude. *The Autobiography of Alice B. Toklas.* New York: Random House, 1933.
———. *Brewsie and Willie.* New York: Random House, 1946.
———. *Four Saints in Three Acts.* New York: Random House, 1934.
———. *Ida: A Novel.* New York: Random House, 1941.
———. *Paris France.* London: Batsford, 1940.
———. *Wars I Have Seen.* New York: Random House, 1945.
———. *What Are Masterpieces.* Los Angeles: Conference, 1940.
Steinbeck, John. *Cannery Row.* New York: Viking, 1945.
———. *The Grapes of Wrath.* New York: Viking, 1939.
———. *In Dubious Battle.* New York: Viking, 1936.
———. *The Moon Is Down.* New York: Viking, 1942.
———. *The Wayward Bus.* New York: Viking, 1947.
Styron, William. *The Long March.* New York: Random House, 1952.
Suckow, Ruth. *The Folks.* New York: Grosset & Dunlap, 1934.
Susman, Warren I. "The Thirties." In *The Development of an American Culture,* edited by Stanley Coben and Lorman Ratner, 179–218. Englewood Cliffs, N.J.: Prentice-Hall, 1970.
Susman, Warren I., ed. *Culture and Commitment, 1929–1945.* New York: George Braziller, 1973.
Swados, Harvey. *A Radical's America.* Boston: Atlantic Monthly Press, 1962.
Swados, Harvey, ed. *The American Writer and the Great Depression.* Indianapolis: Bobbs-Merrill, 1966.
Tanner, Tony. *City of Words: American Fiction, 1950–1970.* New York: Harper & Row, 1971.
Terkel, Studs, ed. *Hard Times: An Oral History of the Great Depression.* New York: Random House, 1970.
Updike, John. "The 50s: Each Man Was an Island," *Newsweek,* 3 January 1994, 36–37.
———. *Rabbit, Run.* New York: Alfred A. Knopf, 1960.
Vidal, Gore. *The City and the Pillar.* New York: E. P. Dutton, 1948.
Vonnegut, Kurt, Jr. *Cat's Cradle.* New York: Holt, Rinehart & Winston, 1963.
———. *Mother Night.* New York: Delacorte, 1966.
———. *Player Piano.* New York: Delacorte/Seymour Lawrence, 1952.
———. *The Sirens of Titan.* London: Victor Gollancz, 1959.
———. *Slaughterhouse-five.* New York: Delacorte, 1969.
Wagner-Martin, Linda. *The Modern American Novel, 1914–1945.* Boston: Twayne, 1989.
Wald, Alan. *The New York Intellectuals: The Rise and Decline of the Anti-Stalinist Left from the 1930s to the 1980s.* Chapel Hill: University of North Carolina Press, 1987.

Waldmeir, Joseph J. *American Novels of the Second World War.* The Hague: Mouton, 1969.

Wandersee, Winifred D. "The Economics of Middle-Income Family Life: Working Women during the Great Depression." In *Decades of Discontent: The Women's Movement, 1920–1940,* edited by Lois Scharf and Joan M. Jensen, 45–58. Westport, Conn.: Greenwood, 1983.

Warren, Robert Penn. *All the King's Men.* New York: Random House, 1946.

Weatherwax, Clara. *Marching! Marching!* New York: International, 1935.

Welty, Eudora. *A Curtain of Green.* New York: Harcourt, Brace, 1941.

———. *Delta Wedding.* New York: Harcourt, Brace, 1946.

———. *The Golden Apples.* New York: Harcourt, Brace, 1949.

———. *Losing Battles.* New York: Random House, 1970.

———. *The Optimist's Daughter.* New York: Random House, 1972.

———. *The Ponder Heart.* New York: Harcourt, Brace, 1954.

———. *The Wide Net.* New York: Harcourt, Brace, 1943.

West, Nathanael. *The Day of the Locust.* New York: New Directions, 1940.

Whyte, William H., Jr. *The Organization Man.* New York: Simon & Schuster, 1956.

Williams, Raymond. *Marxism and Literature.* Oxford: Oxford University Press, 1977.

Wilson, Edmund. *The American Jitters: A Year of the Slump.* 1932. Reprint, Freeport, N.Y.: Books for Libraries, 1968.

Wilson, Sloan. *The Man in the Gray Flannel Suit.* New York: Simon & Schuster, 1955.

Wouk, Herman. *The Caine Mutiny.* Garden City, N.Y.: Doubleday, 1951.

———. *Marjorie Morningstar.* Garden City, N.Y.: Doubleday, 1955.

Wright, Richard. *Black Boy.* New York: Harper, 1945.

———. Introduction to *Never Come Morning,* by Nelson Algren, ix–x. New York: Harper and Brothers, 1942.

———. *Native Son.* New York: Harper & Brothers, 1940.

———. *Savage Holiday.* New York: Avon, 1954.

———. *Uncle Tom's Children.* New York: Harper & Brothers, 1938.

Yerby, Frank. *The Dahomean.* New York: Dial, 1971.

———. *The Foxes of Harrow.* Garden City, N.Y.: Sun Dial, 1947.

———. *The Golden Hawk.* New York: Dial, 1948.

———. *Pride's Castle.* New York: Dial, 1949.

———. *The Saracen Blade.* New York: Dial, 1952.

———. *The Vixens.* New York: Dial, 1947.

———. *A Woman Called Fancy.* New York: Dial, 1951.

Yutang, Lin. *Chinatown Family.* New York: J. Day, 1948.

Index

Wharton, Edith, 30
women characters, 10, 14, 19–24, 28, 35,
    37–41, 71–72, 79–82, 101
women writers, 12, 19–20, 22–24, 28, 41–48,
    78–80, 86–90, 98–108, 110, 131–33
work, 11–20, 30–31, 42, 54–55
World War I, 1, 52, 57, 66, 118
World War II, 40, 49, 53–90, 97, 98, 99, 102–3,
    111, 118, 125–29, 130
Wouk, Herman, 62, 99; *Caine Mutiny, The,* 62;
    Marjorie Morningstar, 99
Wright, Jay, 134

Wright, Richard, 1, 17, 33, 34, 41, 48–49, 51,
    92–97, 133; *Black Boy,* 97; *Native Son,* 17, 33,
    34, 41, 48–49, 92, 94, 97, 98; *Savage Holiday,*
    96–97; *Uncle Tom's Children,* 34
writing style, ix, 1, 16, 21, 24, 33–34, 35, 102

Yerby, Frank, 97–98; *Dahomean, The,* 97; *Foxes
    of Harrow, The,* 97; *Golden Hawk, The,* 97;
    "Health Card," 97; "Homecoming, The,"
    97; *Pride's Castle,* 97; *Saracen Blade, The,* 97;
    Vixens, The, 97; *Woman Cal ed Fancy, A,* 97

The Author

Linda Wagner-Martin is Hanes Professor of English and Comparative Literature at the University of North Carolina at Chapel Hill. The author or editor of 40 books, Wagner-Martin has recently published a biography of Gertrude Stein (*"Favored Strangers": Gertrude Stein and Her Family*) and coedited *The Oxford Companion to Women's Writing in the United States* and its companion anthology, *The Oxford Book of Women's Writing*. The current president of the American literature division of the Modern Language Association, she has been president of the Society for the Study of Narrative, the Ellen Glasgow Society, the Society for the Study of Midwestern Literature, and the Ernest Hemingway Foundation and Society. She has received awards from the Guggenheim Foundation, the National Endowment for the Humanities, the American Council of Learned Societies, the American Philosophical Society, the Bunting Institute, and the Rockefeller Foundation. A past editor of *The Centennial Review*, Wagner-Martin is a member of the editorial boards of a dozen journals. She is currently working on a literary biography of Sylvia Plath.